Complete Guide to
RIGID HEDDLE WEAVING

STACKPOLE BOOKS
An imprint of The Globe Pequot Publishing Group, Inc.
64 South Main Street
Essex, CT 06426
www.globepequot.com

Distributed by NATIONAL BOOK NETWORK
800-462-6420

Original French title: *Guide complet du tissage avec un métier à peigne envergeur*
© 2023, Éditions Eyrolles, Paris, France

All images are from the author © Petra Marciniak, except the following.
Guillaume Médard: p. 10, 13, 46, 50, 84, 96, 99, 101, 103, 107, 109, 111, 113, 115, 117, 119, 121, 123, 125, 127, 129, 131, 133, 135, 137, 139, 141, 143, 145, 151.
Shutterstock: p. 47 TValencia; p. 52, top right, Viktoria Behr; p. 53, top and bottom left, Valkantina.
Diagrams: Maria Ceglia © Éditions Eyrolles: p. 84, 104, 108, 109, 143, 144.

All rights reserved. No part of this book may be reproduced in any form or by any electronic or mechanical means, including information storage and retrieval systems, without written permission from the publisher, except by a reviewer who may quote passages in a review.

The contents of this book are for personal use only. Patterns herein may be reproduced in limited quantities for such use. Any large-scale commercial reproduction is prohibited without the written consent of the publisher.

We have made every effort to ensure the accuracy and completeness of these instructions. We cannot, however, be responsible for human error, typographical mistakes, or variations in individual work.

British Library Cataloguing in Publication Information available

Library of Congress Cataloging-in-Publication Data available

ISBN 978-0-8117-7675-2 (paperback)
ISBN 978-0-8117-7676-9 (ebook)

∞™ The paper used in this publication meets the minimum requirements of American National Standard for Information Sciences—Permanence of Paper for Printed Library Materials, ANSI/NISO Z39.48-1992.

First Edition

Complete Guide to RIGID HEDDLE WEAVING

INCLUDES 11 WEAVING PROJECTS

PETRA MARCINIAK

STACKPOLE BOOKS

Essex, Connecticut
Blue Ridge Summit, Pennsylvania

Contents

Part 1: Basic Techniques 7

The Rigid Heddle Loom 8
Advantages 8
Disadvantages 8
Key Words to Know 8
What Is a Rigid Heddle Loom? 10
Basic Tools 12
Tools to Go Further 13

Yarn 14
A Variety of Materials 14
Yarn Construction 18
Choosing Your Warp Yarn 19
Choosing Your Weft Yarn 19

Calculating Density and Yardage 20
Density 20
Quantity of Yarn Needed 22

Direct Warping 24
Secure the Loom and the Warping Peg 24
Attach Warp to the Back Rod 25
Thread Warp through the Heddle Slots 26
Tie and Cut the Warp 28
Wind Yarn around the Back Warp Beam 29
Thread the Eyes 29
Tie Warp to the Front Rod 31
Even Out the Warp to Start Weaving 32

Weaving with the Rigid Heddle Loom 33
Loading the Shuttles 33
Creating the Shed 34
Weaving 34
Changing Yarn While Weaving 35
Advancing and Winding the Warp 35
Finishing the Weave 36
Removing the Woven Fabric from the Loom 36

When Things Go Wrong 38
Tension Is Not Good 38
Edges Are Not Sharp 38
Weft Is on an Angle 39
Shed Does Not Open Properly 39
Fabric Is Too Stiff or Too Loose 39
Yarn Breaks 40
Length of Fabric Woven Is Difficult to Estimate 42

Finishing Steps 43
Securing the Weave 43
Hemstitch 43
Fringe 46
Washing and Ironing 47
Serger 47
Hems 47
Bias Tape 48
Interfacing 48
Felting 48
Sewing 49

Part 2: Various Weave Structures and Stitches 51

Plain Weave and Variations 52
Playing with Yarn Choice 52
Color Effects 54
Clasped Weft 56
Playing with Weave Effects 57

Focus on the Japanese Saori Technique 60

Other Types of Structures 62
Finger-Controlled Techniques 62
Weaving with a Pick-Up Stick 75
Weaving with Two Heddles 87

Focus on the Norwegian Krokbragd Technique 92
Krokbragd with Two Heddles 93
Krokbragd with a Heddle, a Pick-Up Stick, and a Heddle Rod 94

The detailed Technical Table of Contents is on page 148.

Part 3: 11 Projects to Move Forward in Your Weaving Adventure 97

98 Fringed Scarf

102 Origami Bag

106 Clasped Weft Zippered Pouch

110 Pair of Dish Towels

116 Saori Wall Hanging

120 Light and Airy Wall Hanging

124 Café Curtain

128 Textured Pillow

132 Pair of Placemats

136 Large Woven Trivet

140 Pair of Coasters

Appendices

Glossary 146

Supplies and Resources 147

Bibliography 147

Technical Table of Contents 148

The Author 151

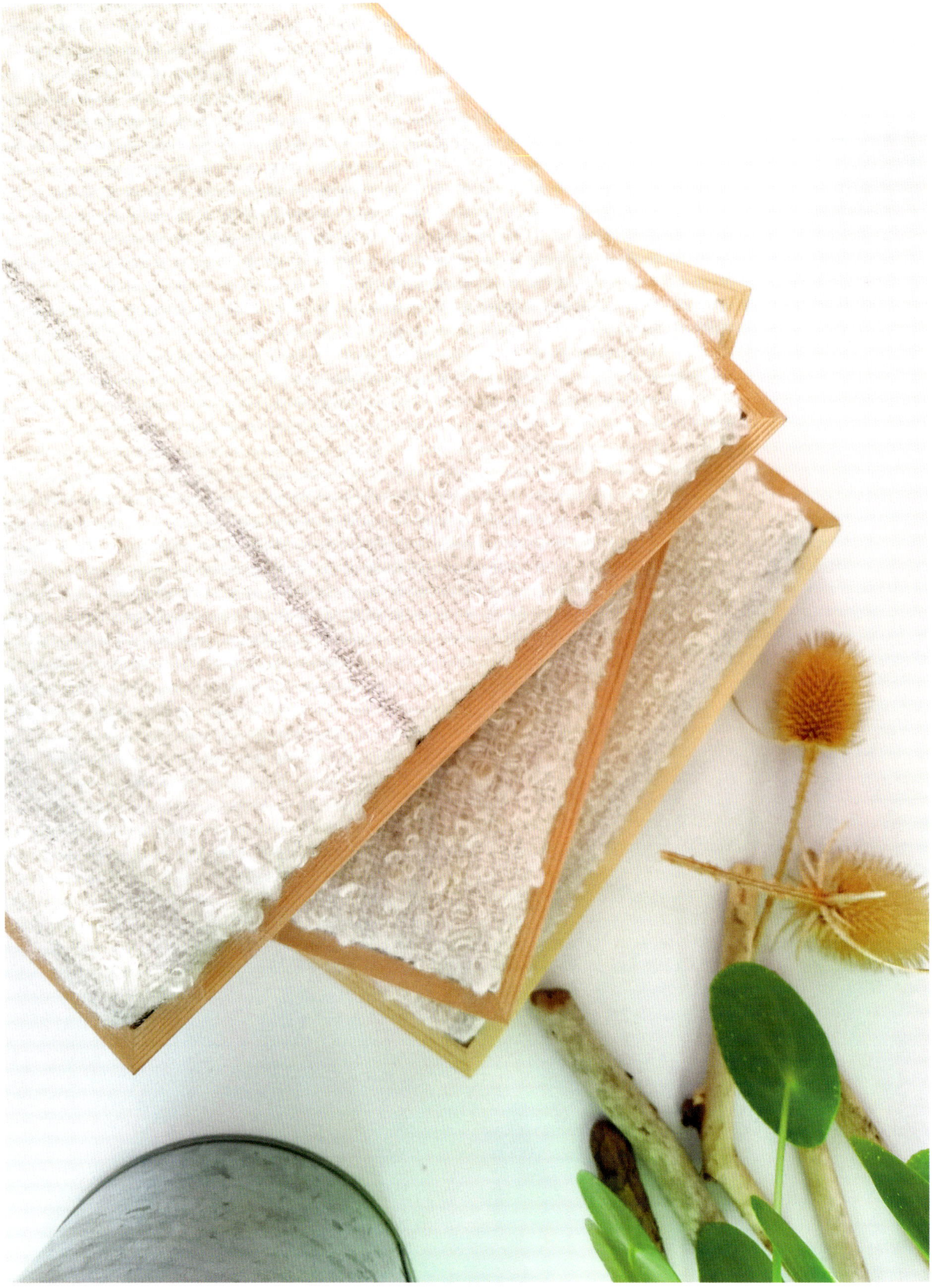

BASIC TECHNIQUES

Weaving is an age-old craft that is pure magic! Seeing a fabric appear simply by interweaving two kinds of threads amazes me as much today as it did the first time I touched a loom.

The possibilities in weaving are endless, and yet they all depend on the same basic principle: align several fibers parallel on a frame, then insert other fibers perpendicularly, passing them sometimes above and sometimes below the threads previously set up. And voilà! You're weaving!

Whether you're an adult or a child, and whether you're looking to make minimalist, utilitarian, sturdy, and practical fabrics, or, on the contrary, to create complex, abstract works of art, just get started and give it a try!

The Rigid Heddle Loom

Weaving has come a long way since the Neolithic period, and many different types of looms have emerged: vertical, horizontal, multi-shaft, rigid heddle, tapestry, and so many other types of looms. There are thousands of them!

Among all this diversity, I consider the rigid heddle loom to be both **the most versatile and the most practical** on the market.

Ignored, misunderstood, or even shunned, it is often wrongly classified as a beginner's loom. Some even say that it's only used for making plain weave (see opposite).

These preconceived notions may keep some from taking the opportunity to rekindle the flame of weaving and to work with a tool that's as effective as it is fun. The rigid heddle loom offers a simple and inexpensive way to learn an ancestral art and make all kinds of fabrics. With it, you can design many types of projects, such as scarves, dish towels, clothing, pillows, and even rugs!

Remember
The rigid heddle loom is a "real" loom—end of discussion!

Advantages

The rigid heddle loom has many positive attributes; here are some of the main ones:

- Weaving with this loom is easy to learn and accessible to all.
- Warping (see page 24) is fast, so you can quickly get started on your project or sample. From the moment you get an idea to the time you start weaving can take as little as one to two hours.
- The rigid heddle loom takes up little space and is lightweight; you can even hang it on a wall to store it.
- It is very affordable.
- It limits yarn loss, leaving room for experimentation.
- You can easily switch from one technique to another as you weave, using the same warp, which is impossible on a "classic" loom. It is easy to start with an openwork pattern, for example, then weave patterns with a pick-up stick in the middle, and finish with a textured pattern.

Disadvantages

Like all looms, this one also has a few weak points.

- Techniques other than plain weave require additional handling or equipment. These are still possible, but generally take much longer than with a shaft loom.
- Yarn tension will never be as satisfactory as on a shaft loom.
- Rigid heddle looms are less stable than conventional shaft looms. This can be a problem if you plan to make large rugs, for example.

Key Words to Know

When starting your weaving adventure, you should know at least these terms below, as they form the basis of weaving in general.

Fabric is created by interweaving two perpendicular threads, the warp and the weft.

Warp: A set of parallel yarns or threads that form the base of the weave. When facing the loom, these are the vertical threads that are stretched in place on the loom first. They are held on the loom under tension between the front and back rollers or beams. The process of installing the warp is called **warping**. Each warp end passes through a slot in the rigid heddle. This heddle makes it possible to lift some threads and lower others in the same movement, allowing the shuttle containing the weft thread to pass through.

Weft: All threads added perpendicularly to the warp (i.e., horizontally when facing the loom) using the **shuttle**, a long piece of wood around which the weft thread is wound. Threads pass either above or below the warp threads, depending on the pattern chosen to form the fabric.

Shed: The opening formed between warp threads. The shuttle containing the weft must pass through this gap.

Plain weave: The most basic of weaving structures. The weft goes systematically "over then under" the warp threads, then the following row does the opposite.

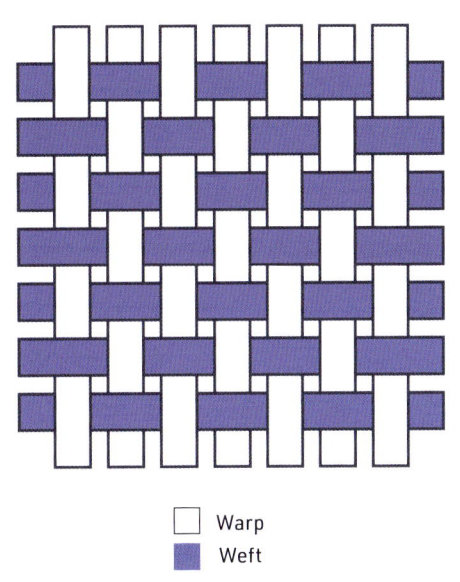

☐ Warp
■ Weft

Classic plain weave

The Rigid Heddle Loom - 9

What Is a Rigid Heddle Loom?

The rigid heddle loom is an intermediate loom between a small frame loom, used mainly to make simple wall hangings (often used in schools for small groups), and the large treadle loom with several shafts.

Like all looms, it has beams for attaching and winding the warp, and a rigid heddle (reed) in the middle to create the pattern and act as a beater for the weft. But unlike "classic" looms, which have at least four shafts, this one has only one.

Rigid heddle looms come in a range of sizes, and some are even foldable. Originally, they were sold to be used on a table, but often a suitable stand is available from the supplier. Admittedly, the stand represents an additional investment, but it brings real comfort if you intend to weave a lot and often. In addition to stabilizing the loom, it allows you to weave both seated and standing, and to put down your shuttles. I highly recommend it.

Front and back rollers or beams: Like multi-shaft looms, the rigid heddle loom includes front and back beams that allow you to weave and wind up lengths of fabric, so that work is not limited by the size of the frame. As you weave, you simply unwind the threads from the warp beam at the back to wind the already woven fabric onto the front cloth beam.

Brakes: The rollers are locked and held in place by brakes. This is a system of a handle with a locking pawl, which is released to advance/wind the just-woven fabric onto the cloth beam.

Front and back rods or bars: Warp sticks are used to attach the warp to the loom. During warping, the warp ends are wound one by one around the back rod or bar before being wound onto the warp beam. In the final step of warping, the warp threads are tied onto the front rod.

Good to Know

Loom notch

Rigid heddle looms generally feature a cutout or notch on the back of the frame. This notch is used to place the loom against the table rather than on top of it, making it possible to weave at an angle, in a more comfortable position.

Rigid heddle (reed): The yarn wound onto the rear warp beam is threaded between the dents of the heddle before being attached to the opposite cloth beam. This rigid heddle has an ingenious system of slots and eyes, acting like two shafts on a floor loom. It is raised or lowered to separate the warp threads; some will go up, others down, depending on the positioning chosen. This creates the space needed to pass the weft thread with the shuttle. As mentioned on page 9, this space is called the "**shed**," and it is located between the heddle and the front beam. The warp ends always alternate between a slot and an eye. Simply manipulating the heddle is enough to shape the weave. It has three functions:

- it determines the **density** of the fabric depending on the spacing of holes in the pattern chosen,
- it creates the **shed** for the weft to pass through,
- it is also used to **beat** the weft pick just completed.

The ingenuity of the system lies in the construction of the heddle's slots and eyes. As the warp ends in the slots move freely, they can be easily manipulated to create patterns more complex than a simple plain weave. These manipulations are made possible by an additional pick-up stick (see page 75).

Different types of heddles are available, with variable spacing between slots and eyes. This allows them to adapt to the thickness of the yarn chosen for the project, and to create different densities. The spacing is marked on the heddle in number of threads per inch (or per 10 cm). For example, a 10-dent reed means that the heddle has slots and eyes for 10 ends per inch (a 40/10 reed has 40 slots/eyes per 10 cm). For a denser fabric, you'll need a 12.5-dent or 12-dent reed with slots and eyes for 12.5 or 12 ends per inch (a 50/10 heddle has 50 slots/eyes per 10 cm).

Inches or Centimeters?

Please note! Most rigid heddle looms give inch indications on the heddle. Always check the unit of measurement before buying a heddle to make sure it suits your needs.

My favorite heddle is the 10-dent (40/10). It is the most versatile and therefore the most suitable for beginners. As the heddle included in most kits is the 8-dent (30/10), I'd advise you to complete your purchase with a 10-dent (40/10) heddle right away. If you plan to use a lot of very fine yarn, a 12.5- or 12-dent (50/10) heddle may come in handy later on.

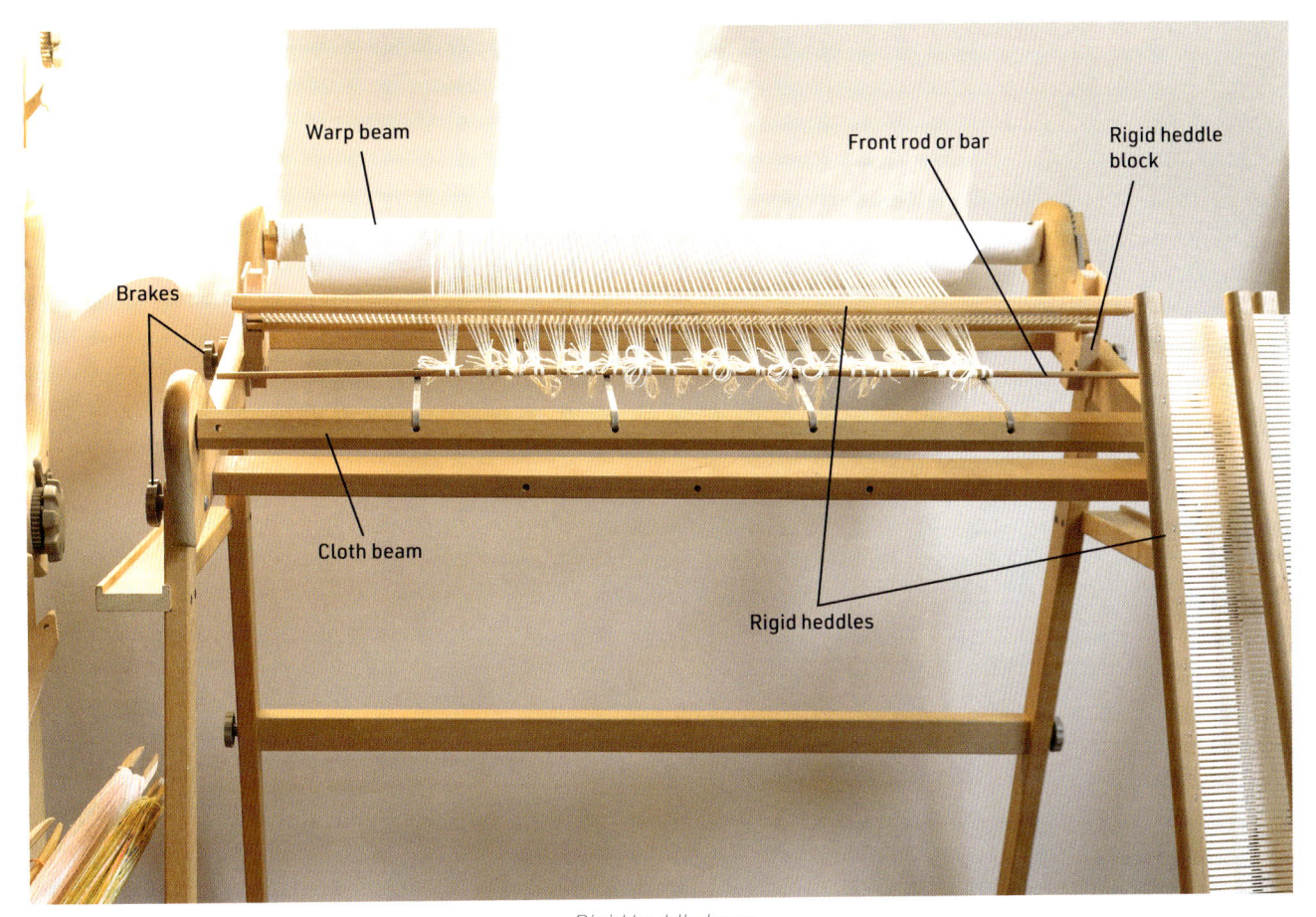

Rigid heddle loom

The Rigid Heddle Loom - 11

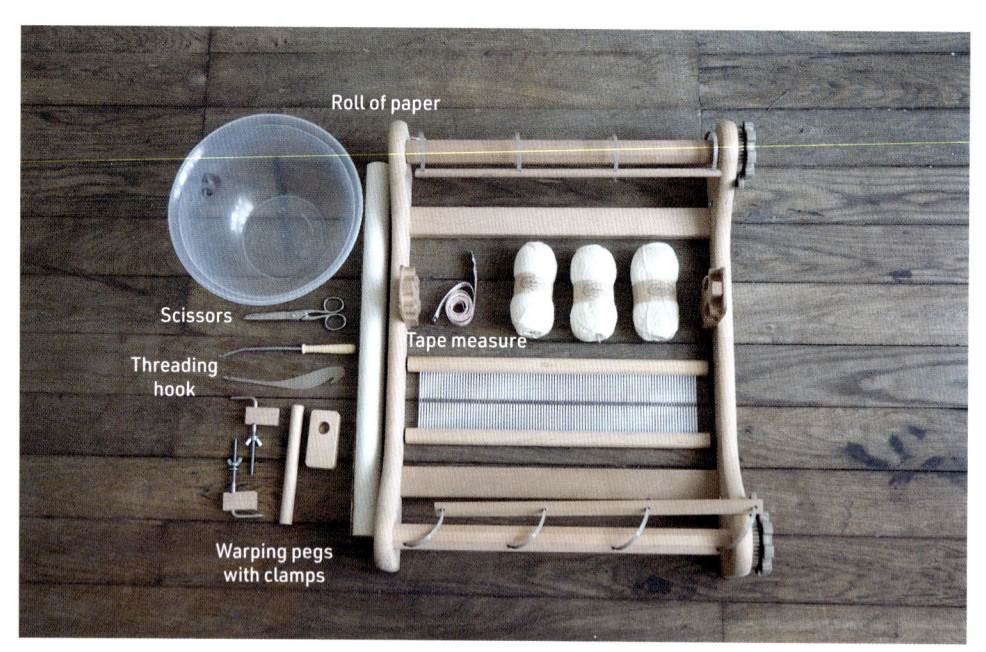

Basic tools

Rigid heddle block: As you pass the weft through the shed, the heddle is held in position by this block. In this way, both hands are free to manipulate the yarn. It can have three different positions:

- up,
- neutral (in the middle),
- down.

To weave, the heddle is positioned alternately on the up and down positions of the block, to create alternating sheds through which to pass the weft. When the heddle is in the up position, the warp ends in the eyes are lifted up, while in the down position, it is the warp ends in the slots that are raised. By moving the heddle from one position to the other, while passing the weft through the shed, the fabric is woven.

The heddle is in the neutral position only when warping or unwinding the yarn from the back warp beam.

Some advanced techniques require the use of two heddles. Rigid heddle blocks on newer rigid heddle looms can usually accommodate two heddles at the same time. For older models, it is often possible to buy spare blocks to accommodate a second heddle.

Basic Tools

A great advantage of weaving with the rigid heddle loom is that, apart from the loom and the fibers, few tools are required. Warping is generally done directly on the loom, so there's no need for a warping machine, warping rods, raddles, or creels.

All you need are these three tools, which are (almost) always included with your rigid heddle loom.

Warping peg with clamps: These are for direct warping; their use is explained on page 24.

Threading hooks: These are used to thread yarn through the heddle during warping. Two different hooks are needed:

- a flat threading hook with a large hook at the end for threading warp ends through the heddle slots.
- a curved threading hook with a small hook at the end for pulling warp ends through the eyes.

Today, you can find both hook types on a single plastic threading hook, but I personally prefer to use two separate threading hooks.

Shuttle: The weft thread is wrapped around the shuttle and passed from one side of the warp to the other through the shed. Flat wooden shuttles are generally used. It's useful to have at least three or four different ones. Choose their size according to the width of your weave. In general, it's best that they be slightly longer than the weave in progress.

In addition to these three tools, you'll also need the following items, which I'm sure you already have somewhere at home:

- a roll of paper (slightly wider than the weave itself, for warping),
- scissors,
- pins,
- tapestry needles for weaving in yarn tails,
- tape measure.

Tools to Go Further

Additional heddles: Other heddles with different densities. To weave with two heddles, you need two heddles with the same density.

Pick-up stick: A flat wooden stick with at least one pointed end. This tool can be used to pick up threads and considerably broaden the range of techniques possible on a rigid heddle loom.

Variable-dent reed: A heddle with sections of varying densities that can be arranged to create different densities within the same warp (see page 57).

Temple: Device used to maintain the warp at its initial width. It is set up between the two selvedges of the fabric.

The possibilities are endless! You can also opt for a wavy shuttle, or a fringe twister to finish off your scarves, etc.

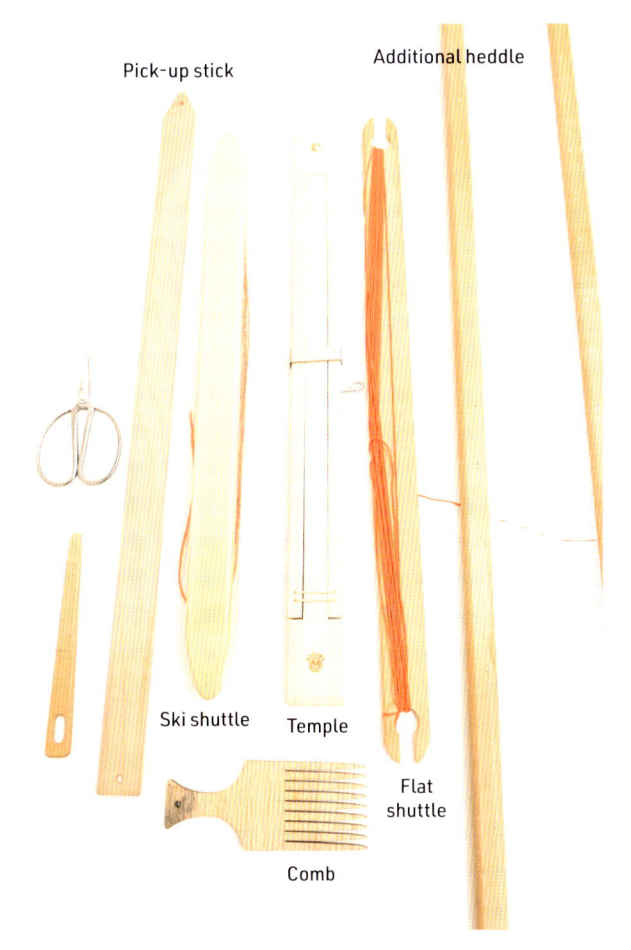

Shuttles and additional tools

Yarn

The success of any weaving depends largely on the ability to choose the right yarn for a project. It determines the quality of the finished fabric. You can make a textile that's strong and sturdy, delicate and flowing, or soft and warm; it is all determined by your warp and weft.

So, before you begin, take the time to ask yourself the following questions:

- For what purpose are you making this fabric? A pillow? scarf? rug? dish towel?
- What are the qualities your fabric should have to be suitable for the project?
  - sturdiness: is it a fabric you'll be sitting or walking on?
  - washability: does it need to be machine-washable?
  - softness: will it be worn close to the body?
  - warmth: should it provide warmth or coolness?
  - fit: does it need to drape or keep its shape?

Your answers to these questions will guide you in your choice of material, yarn construction, and thickness. By playing with these three criteria, you'll end up with a fabric that's just right for your project.

Can I Mix and Match?

You can, of course, use a combination of different fibers in the same item. However, think carefully and make samples to check the resulting material! Every fiber reacts differently to washing. Some shrink a little, others a lot or not at all. The fibers that shrink the most will force the others to follow. The result is often a fabric that puckers and wrinkles everywhere.

So, either make a sample before you start a larger project or at least choose the same fiber for the entire warp and change yarns only in the weft. This second option often proves less problematic, as the yarns are only constricted in one direction.

A Variety of Materials

Wool, cotton, linen, and silk are the most popular fibers for weaving. Spun correctly, they can all be used for both warp and weft.

Natural Fibers of Animal Origin

Wool

In general, this term designates a fiber derived from the fleece of sheep, but its quality varies enormously depending on the breeds used and their region of origin. Indeed, with the numerous breeds of sheep that exist in the world, the various ways of preparing wool, and all the techniques used to spin the strands, you can imagine the diversity of products! Especially since wool can also be made from the fleece of goats and llamas, rabbit hair, etc. The term "wool" used in this book encompasses all these variations.

Wool

Qualities	Disadvantages
• Elastic, holds its shape well • Warm • Supple • Tends to swell after washing, masking irregularities • Repels dirt and moisture • Wrinkle-resistant	• Can felt if not washed properly (avoid rubbing, unsuitable temperature, and/or soap). • Breaks if not twisted enough or if the yarn is single ply. • Does not always drape beautifully, depending on the material from which the wool is produced. • May cause irritation; if in doubt, it's best to test the material before making a garment. • May pill, depending on its thinness and how it was made.

Projects: Warm clothing, rugs, blankets, pillows, scarves.

Superwash, Machine-Washable Wools

Machine-washable wools are chemically treated to prevent felting in the wash. The treatment also reduces the feeling of irritation that the fiber can leave on the skin. The disadvantage, however, is that the yarn loses suppleness and the ability to hold its shape well. These wools deform quite easily, becoming soft and elongated over time.

As we have already seen, wool can also come from the fleece and hair of other animals. Llamas, goats, alpacas, yaks, and rabbits offer beautiful fibers that are often classified in this category. They are like sheep's wool in many respects but have other specific characteristics.

- **Angora goats** produce **mohair**. This is a durable wool, very warm and soft, but also has a very fuzzy halo. Be sure to space the rows of yarn adequately if you want to use it in warp.
- **Alpaca** and **llama** produce a soft, warm wool, but it is not at all as elastic as that of sheep. An item woven with alpaca will be more fluid and less able to keep its shape well than one with sheep's wool.
- **Cashmere** goat's wool is extremely soft, fine, and warm. It tends to be a little breakable and fragile, depending on thickness.
- **Angora rabbits** produce a soft, warm, and very hairy wool. It has virtually no elasticity and does not stand up well to abrasion as a weaving warp, so is best used for weft.
- **Yak** provides a soft, warm, and very light wool, which is one of my favorites; it is definitely something to try with its lovely drape.
- **Horsehair** has been in use for centuries, especially in furniture, for its strength and resistance to abrasion. It is hard-wearing, but not supple, elastic, soft, or warm.

Silk

Silk is one of the most luxurious fibers in existence. It is produced by a caterpillar commonly known as a silkworm. Silk is actually the "slime" of this caterpillar, which creates its cocoon before transforming into a moth. It coils up in its saliva, which hardens into this fiber. To access the fiber, the cocoon is plunged into boiling water a few days after it is formed, killing the worm, and then the silk can simply be unwound. Between 750 and 1,300 yards of continuous thread can be recovered from a single cocoon! This first thread is often beige. The silk at this stage is called "**raw silk**," and fabric made from it looks more like linen than silk. Most often, raw silk is cleaned, bleached, refined, and dyed to become the soft, shiny, supple fiber we know today.

Silk

There are several types of silk available on the market today.

- Mulberry silk is made from a thread produced by the *Bombyx mori*, or mulberry silkworm. These silkworms live exclusively in captivity and are bred in China, Japan, and India. The caterpillars feed exclusively on mulberry leaves and produce the finest quality silk available. The thread is also extremely long.
- Tussah silk, also known as "wild silk," is harvested from worms that are not in captivity but live in the wild. The fiber produced from their filaments is thicker and more uneven. Shantung silk falls into this category, among others.
- Bourette silk, or schappe silk, is obtained from the remnants of filaments left over from silk combing and carding, to which the usual treatment cannot be applied because the threads are too short. It differs from raw silk in that it is more matte, irregular, and supple.
- Éri silk is also known as "peace silk," as it is not necessary to kill the silkworm to obtain the fiber. The moth leaves the cocoon after spinning. The beauty of its variegated color comes from the plants it feeds on. This is the silk I prefer. I love its less shiny appearance and especially its slightly rustic feel. This differs from mulberry silk, which I find to be rather slippery.

Qualities	Disadvantages
• Strong • Soft • Beautiful drape • Supple • Shiny • Very smooth • Can retain a third of its weight in moisture without feeling wet • Temperature regulating	• Fluid, but virtually no resilience or elasticity • Expensive • Often very thin • Often slippery

Projects: Scarves, summer tops

Natural Fibers from Plants

Cotton

Cotton is a fiber that comes from the cotton plant, a shrub that produces the cotton bolls used to make cotton. It is a low-growing plant with high water consumption. In its natural state, cotton is rather matte, but today there are many "mercerized" cottons on the market. These cottons are passed through a caustic soda bath to make them stronger, brighter, and easier to dye. However, mercerization also makes them less absorbent, and therefore less suitable for certain projects (dish towels, for example).

Cotton

Unmercerized cotton is very durable, hard-wearing, and absorbs moisture well. It has virtually no elasticity. The fabric does not provide warmth, like wool, but rather coolness, which is perfect for summer wear.

Qualities	Disadvantages
• Strong and durable. • Easy to work with. • Can be machine-washed in hot water. • Brings a coolness to textiles. • Smooth. • Slightly elastic. • Inexpensive.	• Tends to shrink in the wash. • Not warm. • Wrinkles easily. • Requires a lot of water and pesticides.
Projects: Summer clothing, household linens, summer pillows.	

Flax (Linen)

Flax is very rustic-looking, decorative, and easy to grow.

Its stems are used to make linen threads. It is a very stable, stiff, and absorbent material, but has no elasticity. Linen has a certain sheen (depending on treatment). Fabrics created with linen have a lovely drape and a cool, slightly rough feel.

Qualities	Disadvantages
• Holds up well to washing, becomes softer with each wash and ironing. • Absorbs moisture very well. • Beautiful drape. • Can be machine-washed in hot water. • Brings coolness to textiles. • Stiff. • Smooth. • Comes from a plant that can be produced in many climates.	• Not at all elastic and not very resistant to friction wear during weaving, which can make the weaving rather tricky. Best used in warp if you are a beginner. • Tends to shrink in the wash. • Not warm. • Wrinkles easily.
Projects: Summer clothing, household linens, summer pillows, rugs, placemats, table runners, curtains.	

Linen and hemp

Hemp

Hemp is made from the plant of the same name. This fiber is coming back into fashion because it is quick and easy to grow, requiring little maintenance, fertilizer, or water

Yarn - 17

(unlike cotton, for example). Hemp is rustic and rough, but also very robust, and its natural look blends well with modern interiors.

Qualities	Disadvantages
• Very durable. • Absorbs moisture well. • Antibacterial. • Can be machine-washed in hot water. • Brings freshness to textiles. • Stiff. • Comes from a plant that can be grown in many climates.	• Very tedious transformation process. • Difficult to obtain soft fibers. • Not at all elastic. • Not warm.
Projects: Summer clothing, household linens, summer pillows, rugs, placemats, table runners, curtains.	

Artificial and Synthetic Fibers

Artificial fibers are mostly derived from the cellulose found in certain plants (eucalyptus and bamboo, for example), which is chemically transformed.

Synthetic fibers, on the other hand, are derived from petroleum or coal. They are man-made through chemical synthesis or polymerization.

These fibers are the most widely used in the textile industry, but are rarely used in artisanal weaving, so I won't dwell on them here. This is because, despite their qualities (low absorbency, high strength, wrinkle-resistance, low cost, easy to dye, unaffected by sunlight, and machine-washable), these yarns require a great deal of energy resources, which makes their production highly polluting (both in terms of the process of transformation into textile fibers and the significant consumption of water).

Infinite Possibilities

Just a few years ago, we would have only listed wool, silk, linen, cotton, and even synthetic yarns as choices for weaving, but it is actually possible to weave with any material or fiber you fancy.

This is one of the things that fascinates me most about weaving! You can think outside the box and use, for example:

- metallic fibers,
- plastic bags cut into strips,
- leather,
- branches,
- paper,
- fabrics.

Don't limit yourself—explore and play with whatever you can get your hands on! You'll see that it adds a whole new dimension to weaving.

Yarn Construction

Raw fibers must be spun to be transformed into yarns of different thicknesses. Yarns are made up of:

- several strands twisted together to form a single thread,
- or a single strand, called "singles" or "single ply" yarn.

The number of strands used to make a yarn says nothing about its **thickness**: a yarn made with two thick strands may be much thicker than a yarn made with eight thin strands.

On the other hand, the number of strands generally gives an indication of the yarn's **durability**. A yarn made from several strands is stronger than a single ply yarn. The latter is generally not recommended for the warp, especially if you're just starting out.

Choosing Your Warp Yarn

The best warp yarns, and the easiest for beginners to work with, are those that hold up to the tension on the loom and to the continual friction produced by beating (pulling the heddle toward you after each weft pick to beat it into place) and those that don't catch on each other, so that the shed can always open properly.

The yarn must therefore be:

- strong,
- well-twisted,
- fairly smooth,
- somewhat elastic.

Threads that are too hairy or fancy (bouclé or with sequins, beads, bits of fabric, and the like) risk snagging on each other as the shed moves, which can spoil the fun of weaving, especially for beginners. To limit this problem, you should space them further apart or alternate them with other smoother fibers.

Overly elastic fibers, such as certain superwash merino wools, are also unsuitable for warping. Although pleasant to work with during weaving, they result in a fabric that shrinks and ripples like an accordion as soon as it leaves the loom.

Choosing Your Weft Yarn

As the weft is not under tension during weaving and does not have to endure constant friction from the heddle, weft yarns are less stressed. You can therefore use less twisted yarns or hairy yarns, as well as less "conventional" materials, such as metal threads, leather, etc.

So have fun, play around, experiment, bearing in mind that the weft influences 50% of the quality of the final fabric. For example, if you want a soft, flowing scarf, hemp may not be the best choice.

Yarn Tension Test

To find out whether a yarn will withstand the tension exerted by the loom, perform these two tests before the work begins.

1. Take a good length of yarn between the thumb and forefinger of each hand and pull in short bursts.

2. Try to stretch it slowly and evenly.

Yarn that breaks cleanly on the first test or tears on the second will probably behave in the same way once on the loom. It is therefore inadvisable to use it as a warp, at least for your first attempts.

Calculating Density and Yardage

> **Quote**
> "It is the relationship between the thread, the structure, and the density that determines the success of the planned weaving project."
> Betty Briand, *The Art of Weaving*
> (Stackpole Books, 2023)

Once you have chosen your yarn, all you need to do is decide on the density of your fabric and calculate how much material you'll need.

This chapter may seem a little serious, and you may be tempted to move straight on to the next chapter, but don't do it! The calculations and explanations given here will make all the difference in helping you successfully complete your projects and give you a real understanding of weaving. Knowing how to handle the subtleties of density is the key to successful weaving.

Density

Density is the number of warp and/or weft threads per inch, also known as the sett. Warp density is determined by the rigid heddle (reed) selected, and weft density by how you beat.

> **Remember**
> For the rigid heddle loom, warp density is determined by the size of the heddle you will be working with: 10 dent? 12 dent? Go to page 11 to refresh your memory.

Density hugely impacts the fabric you create. It influences the drape, durability, and feel of the fabric. If you use too many threads in the warp you'll end up with a stiff, rigid fabric. With too few, you'll get an unstable, flowing fabric.

These effects can, of course, be deliberate. For example, you wouldn't choose the same density for an upholstery fabric as for a summer scarf.

Nevertheless, before considering this question of use, the first thing to do is always to calculate the "ideal density" of your yarn, the one that would enable you to obtain a balanced, stable fabric that's pleasant to the touch. Only once you've estimated this can you revise your calculation to suit your project.

Calculating Ideal Yarn Density

The aim is to calculate the optimum number of warp threads to use per inch.

1. Wrap the yarn you've chosen for your project around a piece of cardboard or a ruler, carefully keeping the strands side by side, with no gaps or overlapping.

2. For greater precision, wrap the thread around the cardboard to form a 2-inch-wide band. Record the number of wraps you've made by counting the number of strands in your row. For example, it may take 40 wraps or 40 strands to make a 2-inch row.

3. Divide this number by 2 to find the number of wraps (ends) per 1 inch. In this example, 40 ÷ 2 = 20 ends per 1 inch.

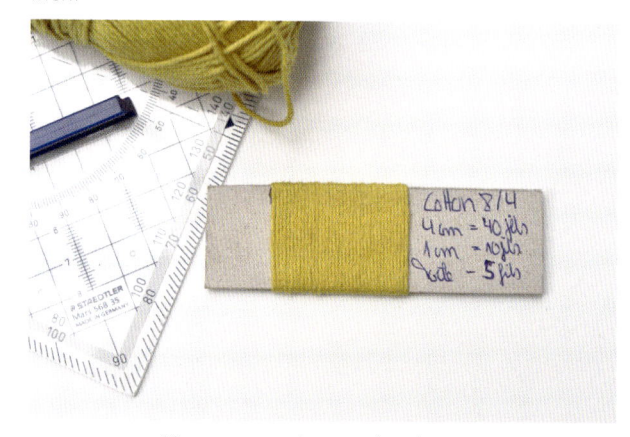

Yarn wrapped around a piece of cardboard to calculate density.

This number indicates the ideal density for a fabric measuring 1 × 1 in., i.e., **warp AND weft** together. As you want to calculate only the warp density here, you must again divide this figure taking into account the structure of your weave:

- for a plain weave, you'll need to divide this number by 2 (so, 10 ends per inch for the example given),
- for a twill (which isn't very common with the rigid heddle loom), you'll need to multiply it by ⅔ (so, about 13.3 ends per inch for this example).

In our example, the ideal yarn density is 10 ends per inch (often abbreviated epi) for plain weave. So you'll need to use a 10-dent rigid heddle for your first tests.

Adapting Yarn Density According to Certain Criteria

Calculating the ideal density is a first step in enabling you to choose the density of your fabric and the corresponding heddle. But there are other factors to consider that may increase or decrease this density.

Fabric Function

How will my fabric be used? Will it be for upholstery or clothing? Depending on function, you can increase or reduce the number of ends per inch calculated in the previous step and adapt it to the type of fabric you're looking for.

- For fabrics requiring some fluidity, such as a scarf, reduce the density by 5% to 10%.
- For firmer, more durable, and solid materials, such as upholstery fabrics, increase the density by 15% to 20%.

Yarns Used

The type of yarn you use also influences your choice of density. For example, if you're using mohair, a fine, very hairy yarn, you'll need to space the warp ends farther apart than if you're using a smooth, slippery silk, even if both yarns have the same number of wraps on your ruler.

- For slippery yarns, increase the density slightly to avoid an unstable fabric.
- For wool, which swells much more after washing than any other fiber, reduce the density by 10% to 15%.

Weave Structure

The weave, or weave structure, will also determine the choice of density. Plain weave, for example, is a structure in which all threads are systematically interwoven, generally resulting in a stiffer fabric. In twill, on the other hand, the weft passes over and under two or three warp ends; there is less interlacing, so the finished fabric is more fluid.

If you use the same yarn for both plain and twill, you'll need to adjust the density.

- For plain weave, you'll need to reduce the density; otherwise the frequent interlacing won't leave much room for the weft.
- For twill, which involves less interlacing, there's more room for the weft, so you can warp the yarn closer together.

You'll need to reduce the number of wraps per inch counted on your ruler to one-half that amount for plain weave and to two-thirds of that number for twill.

Checking Density with a Sample

All the above calculations and considerations give you an idea of how to obtain a fabric suited to your project, depending on the yarn you've chosen. But this is only theory. Once you've got a clearer picture of the material and the desired look, there's only one way to choose the right density for your fabric: sampling.

Like the calculation stage, this is a step we'd gladly dispense with to save time. Yet it's the only way to confirm the quality of your fabric and end up with a final project you'll like.

Here are the different stages of sampling:

1. Weave a piece at least 6 inches wide and long.
2. Remove it from the loom.
3. Wash it, adapting the cleaning to suit the type of yarn used, as you would for the finished project.
4. Lay the piece flat to dry completely.

Only after all these steps will you be able to judge your fabric. Yes, it is time consuming. But the washing stage can have a major impact on your fabric and is essential for checking the end quality. This stage will also enable you to measure the shrinkage to be taken into account on your actual project. Without this information, you run the risk of ending up with a piece that is far too small or too short or, on the contrary, too floppy and not able to hold its shape.

Remember

The most important thing in choosing the right density is always to make samples! Sample, sample, sample!

Quantity of Yarn Needed

To calculate the quantity of yarn needed for your project, first determine the following two figures:

- the density (see page 20): e.g., 10 ends per inch,
- the dimensions of your weave, taking into account all forms of shrinkage.

Calculating Shrinkage

Shrinkage is the reduction in the width and length of the fabric. There are two types of shrinkage to be considered in this calculation.

Weaving Shrinkage and Loom Waste

The greatest shrinkage in width is due to the weaving process itself, representing around 2% to 8% less material. On your first attempts, you'll quickly notice that the edges of your piece are difficult to manage: too loose and curled, or too tight, which reduces the width of the weave and is the most common case. You'll find some tips on how to avoid this on page 38.

Of course, we try to avoid this shrinkage as much as possible, but a slight reduction in the width is virtually inevitable, especially when you're just starting out. Take this shrinkage into account when determining the dimensions when warping your loom. In any case, you risk losing from 2% to 8% in width, depending on your experience and the yarn you use. To compensate for this shrinkage, always allow for an inch or so of width by adding warp ends when warping the loom.

The loss of yarn in length is quite substantial and frustrating in weaving, representing between 16 and 24 inches from each of the warp ends. As this loss is largely due to the construction and operation of the loom, you can't really do much about it. It's impossible, for example, to weave between the back rod and the 4 inches before the heddle. Although it varies, this distance is generally around 8 to 12 inches of yarn. If you're making a scarf, you can use part of it as fringe, but the rest of the yarn will be lost. The same applies to the front knots: unless you use them as fringe, they are lost threads.

In any case, always add at least 16 inches of warp to the total length of your project to make sure you have enough yarn.

Processing Shrinkage

Most woven fabrics will undergo a second form of shrinkage, one that is caused by washing and subsequent handling.

This shrinkage depends entirely on the material and the care given to it, so it's difficult to give a general figure here. The only way to calculate it is to make a sample! Ah yes, sorry.

Some fabrics won't change much, but others will lose 4 to 6 inches. If you haven't anticipated this, the difference can make the fabric unusable.

How It Works

Here's how to account for the shrinkage of a weave, still using the example on page 20, and an estimated density of 10 ends per inch. The dimensions of the finished fabric will be 16.5 inches wide by 70 inches long.

When setting up the warp, estimate the lengths of yarn where they cannot be woven and add this figure to the length of yarn planned for your project. In this example, the unused warp length is 16 inches. You'll need a warp at least 86 inches long (70 inches + 16 inches).

For the weft, measure the width of the yarn strands in the heddle after warping, then compare it with the width of the cut, washed, and dried sample. In this example, the weft width has been reduced from 16.5 to 15 inches, so we've lost about 9% of material. To end up with a project that is 16.5 inches, we'll need to warp at least 18 inches of yarn (16.5 + 9%).

Knowing that the warp threads will need to be 86 inches long and the weft 18 inches wide, you can now calculate the length of yarn required.

Calculating the Length of Yarn Required

To illustrate the calculations required for this estimate, let's take the same example of a fabric with a density of 10 ends per inch, which will need to be 18 inches wide by 86 inches long for a finished project measuring 16.5 × 70 inches.

For the Warp

To determine the number of threads to be warped, calculate: **density × width of the piece**. In this example: 10 ends per inch × 18 inches = 180 warp ends.

To determine the length of the warp ends, calculate: **number of warp ends × length of warp ends required for weaving**. In this example: 180 ends × 86 inches = 430 yards of yarn required.

For the Weft

To determine the number of weft picks, perform the following calculation: **density × length of piece**. In this example: 10 ends per inch × 86 inches = 860 threads to weave the 86 inches.

To determine the length of the weft yarn, calculate: **number of weft picks × width of piece**. In this example: 860 threads × 18 inches = 430 yards of yarn required.

In Conclusion

For the example detailed here, which would produce a finished piece measuring 16.5 inches × 70 inches with a density of 10 ends per inch, the quantity of yarn required is 430 yards of yarn for the warp and 430 yards of yarn for the weft.

Calculating Density and Yardage - 23

Direct Warping

Once you've chosen your project, your yarn, and completed all the calculations needed, it is time to put the warp onto the loom. This operation is called warping.

Though there are two ways to warp the loom, direct warping and indirect warping, I only use the first with the rigid heddle loom as it is much simpler and faster.

Materials Required
Included in the rigid heddle loom kit
- Loom
- Heddle
- Warping peg
- 2 clamps
- Flat threading hook

Additional materials
- Curved metal threading hook
- Yarn
- Scissors
- Bowl
- Roll of paper
- Tape measure

Secure the Loom and the Warping Peg

1 Secure the loom to a table using a clamp. Be sure to immobilize the back of the loom using the notches on the sides.

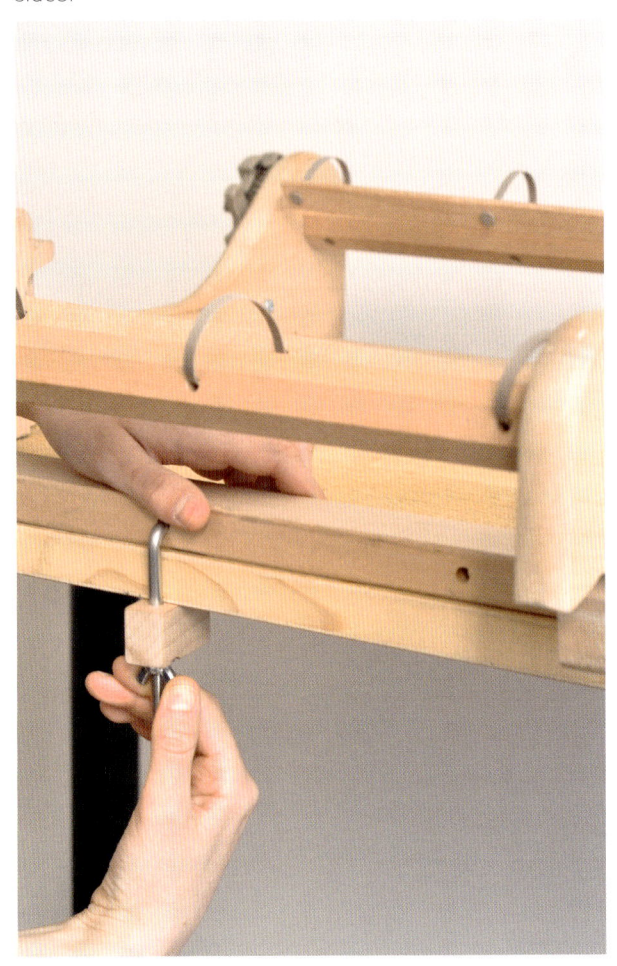

2 Secure the warping peg to a chair or stool opposite the loom. The distance between the two should match the length of warp to be prepared.

Attach Warp to the Back Rod

3 Place the ball of warp in a bowl under the table and tie the end around the back rod or bar with a double knot. Tie it to the right side of the bar, about where you want the edge of your future weaving to be. You will continue warping to the left of this knot.

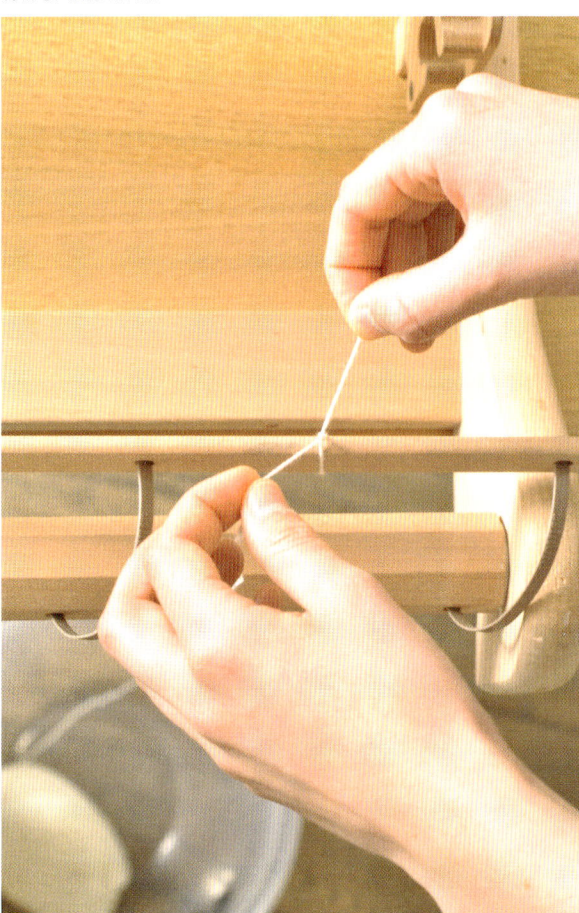

4 Once the warp is in place, the weave should be centered on the loom. To position it correctly, calculate the length that should be left on either end of the rod stick, subtract the width of the desired fabric (10 inches, for example) and divide the figure by 2. So, if the rod measures 16 inches, calculate 16 inches − 10 inches = 6 inches, divided by 2. You'll need to leave 3 inches before the first knot for the weave to be centered.

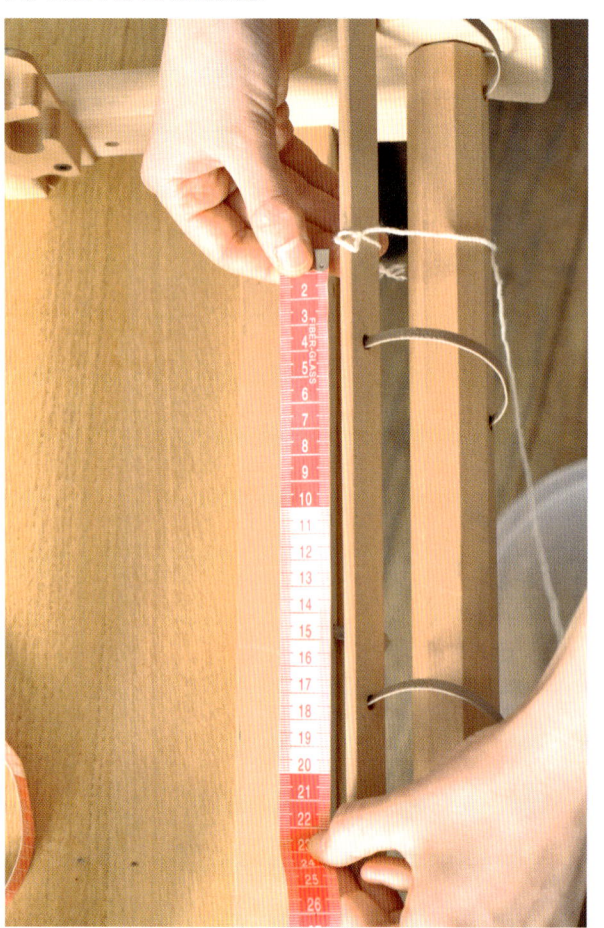

Thread Warp through the Heddle Slots

5 Stand in front of the loom and insert the flat threading hook through the slot that is most in front of your starting knot. Hook the yarn and pull it toward you.

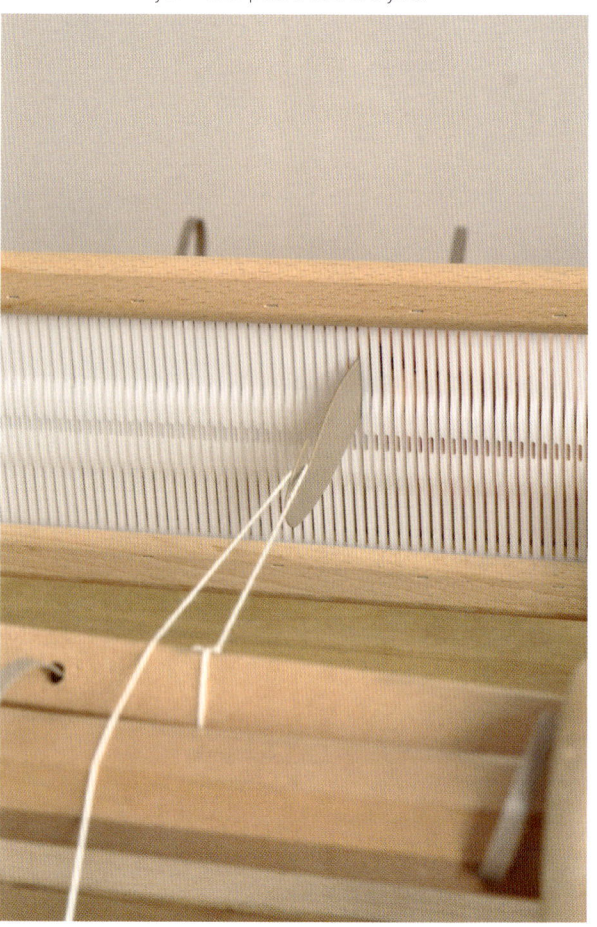

26 - Complete Guide to Rigid Heddle Weaving

6 Pull the thread all the way to the warping peg attached to a chair or stool in step 2, and slide the thread around the peg.

7 Insert the threading hook into the next slot toward the center of the weaving. First wrap the warp thread around the rod or bar, then pull it through the slot. Bring the thread up to the warping peg on the chair or stool and slide it around the peg.

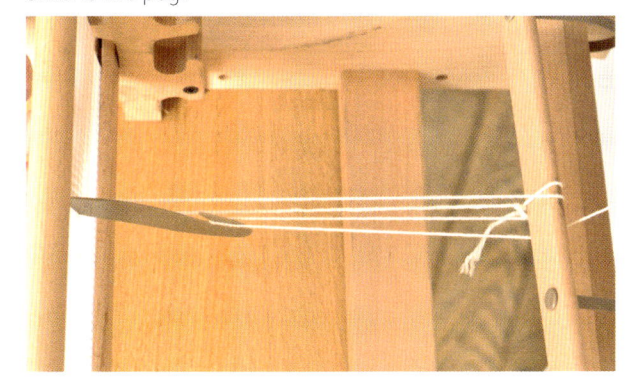

8 Continue in this manner until you've reached the width you need for your project, taking into account the fabric density you've chosen.

Notes

When you grab the thread with the threading hook, every other warp end will alternate coming from above or below the rod. This is normal, so take them as they come.

Likewise, make sure you go from one slot to the next, without leaving any empty.

Push down the threads you've slipped around the warping peg so they don't escape.

Direct Warping - 27

Tie and Cut the Warp

9 Continue warping the slots until you've reached the desired width. To be sure, measure the distance between the first and last thread using a tape measure.

10 Take a strand of yarn in a different color and tie the bunch of warp threads together with a double knot, about 12 inches from the warping peg.

11 Using scissors, cut the loop around the peg down the middle.

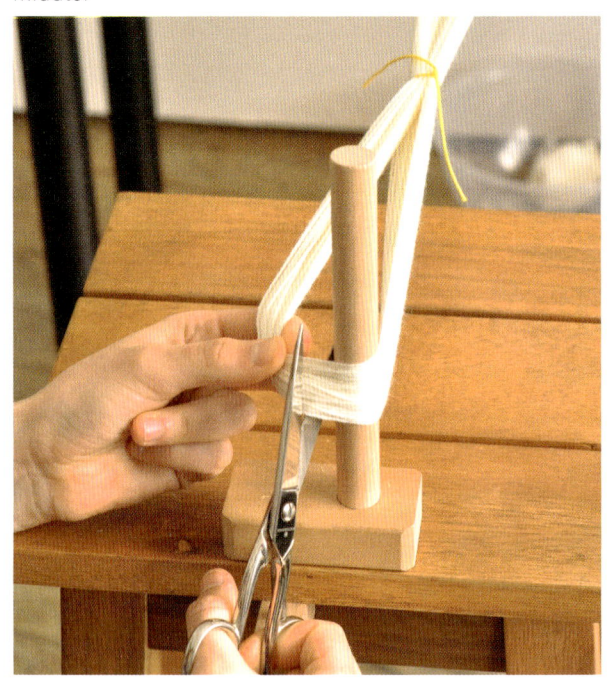

12 Keep the threads taut in your hand.

You will no longer need the warping peg and the clamp that holds it in place.

28 - Complete Guide to Rigid Heddle Weaving

Wind Yarn around the Back Warp Beam

13 To wind the yarn, it must be under tension. It's best if you can get someone to hold the warp in front of the loom while you wind it on. If you're on your own, however, you can weight the threads down with a bottle or a weight.

- Take the paper roll and slide the end of it under the yarn so that it wraps around the warp beam. This will separate the warp ends and prevent them from catching on each other.

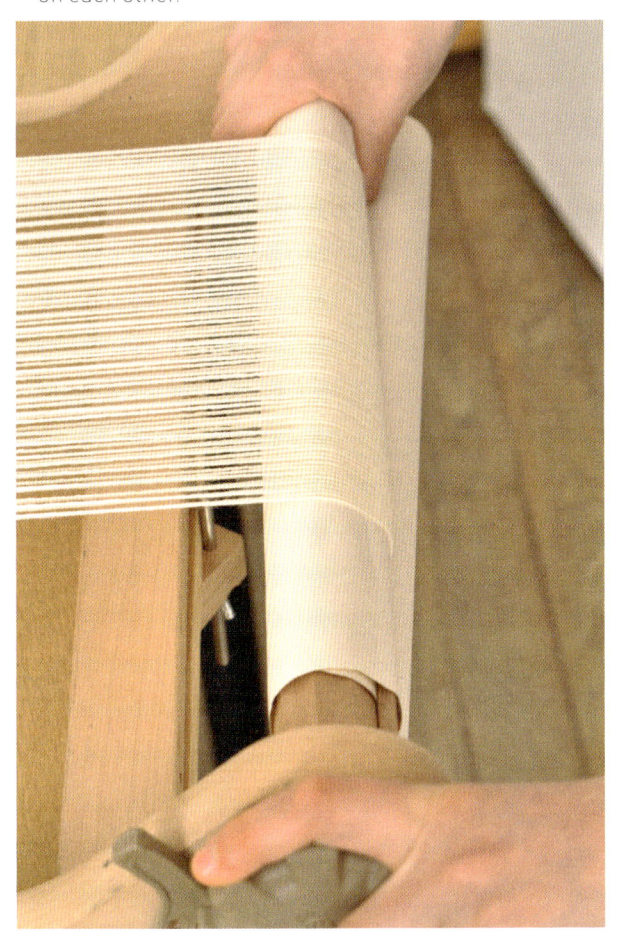

- Start turning the warp beam and wind the warp threads around it.
- Continue to wind until about 12 inches of yarn remain on the front of the loom.

- Remove the colored thread holding the yarn together.
- You can also remove the clamp holding the loom in place.

The front of your loom should look like the photo below.

There are 2 threads in each slot, which you'll need to separate in the next step.

Thread the Eyes

14 Using the metal threading hook, pick up the 2 warp ends in the first slot on the right and move them around a little to see which is furthest to the right on the back beam. This right-hand thread is the one to be moved into the eye. Drop the left-hand thread: you don't need to move it, as it's already well positioned in the slot.

Direct Warping - 29

15 Keep tension on the right-hand warp end you are holding and slide it upward until it is above the eye, continuing to keep it under tension.

16 Now insert the metal threading hook, with the hook facing up, **into the eye to the right of the slot** to catch the warp thread just behind the heddle. As the threading hook is slightly leaning to the right, you should be able to catch the strand without having to look behind the heddle. It may take a few tries before you master the technique, but don't be discouraged. With a little practice, you'll get the hang of it.

17 Once you've caught the thread, pull it through the eye. Place the 2 warp ends (the one left in the slot and the one now through the eye) over to the right, so as to differentiate them from the strands still to be separated.

18 Continue in this way across the whole row, until you've separated all the double strands in slots. You now have one thread in each slot and each eye.

Tie Warp to the Front Rod

19 Take the warp ends in the first 4 slots and the first 4 eyes, then divide them into two groups. In each group are 2 warp ends from slots and 2 warp ends from eyes.

20 Bring the two groups of yarn over and around the front rod or bar, as shown in the photo.

21 Tie the two groups of threads together to form a bow tie, as with shoelaces.

22 Continue in this way with all the yarn, taking care to maintain an even tension across the whole row.

Even Out the Warp to Start Weaving

The actual warping is now finished and the loom should look like this: one thread through each slot and eye, all tied tightly to the front rod.

Check that you have **balanced tension** across all the warp ends. If some parts are looser than others, you can adjust the tension by retightening.

However, large gaps are still visible in the warp, and it is impossible to start weaving with these "holes."

23 So take a thick yarn and weave back and forth about 6 times **WITHOUT** beating (see page 33). Wait to beat until after weaving the 6 passes. This requires a little force, as all the threads must be pushed down together toward the bottom. But this movement will even out the layer of warp, as if by magic. At the end, when your weave has been cut from the loom, you can remove this thick yarn.

This is what your loom should look like before you can finally begin your project. The warp tension is even and there are no gaps.

All you need to do now is prepare your shuttles with the weft, and you're ready to discover the pleasures of weaving!

Weaving with the Rigid Heddle Loom

Loading the Shuttles

On my rigid heddle loom, I use only wooden stick shuttles. They are the easiest to use, are inexpensive, and you can fill them much more than any other type of shuttle. What's more, you don't need any other equipment to fill them, unlike boat shuttles, for example, which require the use of a very, very expensive bobbin winder.

It is true that stick shuttles don't empty automatically like boat shuttles do; you always have to manually remove the required amount of yarn before each weft pass. This requires a little time and patience, but the advantages outweigh the disadvantages.

Contrary to what you might think, the yarn is not simply wrapped around the stick shuttle to fill it. This would create an extra thickness in the middle of the shuttle that would make it difficult to pass through the shed. To prepare it correctly, the yarn is wound on in a figure-8 style following the steps listed below.

1 Take your shuttle so that you have its H-shape in front of you and wrap the end of the yarn once around the notch to secure it a little, without tying a knot.

2 Hold the yarn with your fingers to prevent it escaping. Start winding the weft thread onto the shuttle, forming a figure 8 around the bar to the right of the notch by placing the yarn in the top notch and then the bottom one, always crossing the yarn over the right-hand edge of the shuttle.

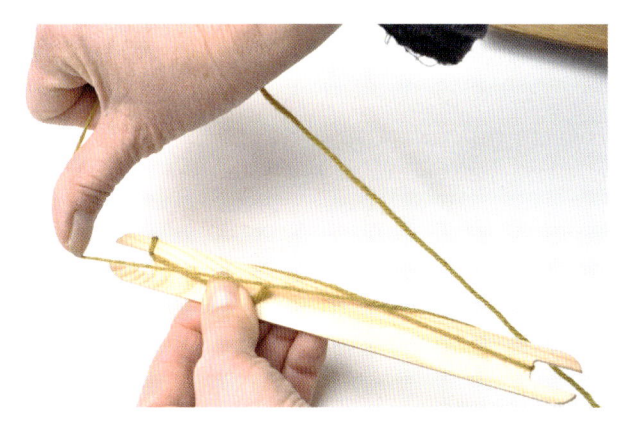

3 Once the right-hand side of the shuttle has been filled, turn it so that the left-hand side is on the right, and proceed as in step 2.

4 Once you've filled both edges of this side of the shuttle, turn it over so that the back is in front of you, and do the same thing: first make figure 8s to fill the right side, then turn the shuttle to fill the left side.

5 Once all four sides have been filled, finish by winding the yarn in the middle a few times.

You will end up with a full but virtually flat shuttle, which will go into the shed without too much trouble.

It is best to choose a shuttle that's long enough to be able to pass it easily from one side of the weft to the other. Unwind a short length of yarn before inserting it into the shed, one long enough to cover the width of the weft, but short enough to avoid tangling and snagging.

Creating the Shed

To pass the weft thread between the warp threads, we need to create a space. This space is **the shed**. In the case of a rigid heddle loom, this shed is created by the heddle block position. Up and down positions are alternated to allow the shuttle yarn to pass between the warp threads and weave through them.

When the heddle is in the up position in the block, the warp ends threaded through the eyes are lifted up. In the "down" position, the warp ends in the eyes are at the bottom. The threads in the eyes are **active**, as they are the ones you move when alternating the position of the heddle. Slot warp ends are inactive, as they remain motionless. It is very important to know this when using advanced techniques, as it is because of this particular feature that more complex patterns can be created by again separating these "inactive" threads.

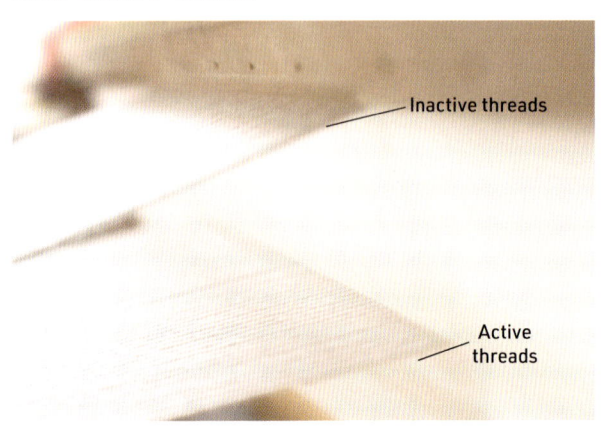

Weaving

Once you've familiarized yourself with the movement of the heddle, weave your first row of weft.

1 Place the heddle in the up position, unwind the shuttle yarn a little and pass it through the shed from right to left. As the shuttle thread is not yet attached to the weave, make sure that the end of the thread remains outside the warp. Once the shuttle has emerged on the left, gently pull the weft thread until a tail of only about 2 inches is outside the first warp thread.

2 To hide this tail, wrap it around the first warp thread. Tuck it into the shed parallel to the first woven thread for ½ inch and pull the remainder down below the weave. The end that protrudes at the back is secure, as it is integrated into the weave. It can be trimmed with scissors when the weaving is finished.

3 With the heddle, beat the weft just inserted and then set the heddle in its down position.

4 Repeat steps 1 and 3, passing the shuttle from one side of the warp to the other before beating with the heddle.

Remember
"Pass, beat, change position" should become your mantra!

Practice until this movement becomes automatic and you no longer need to think about each pass.

When weaving, it's very important to find a certain consistency. The movement is repetitive and rhythmic. Once you've found this rhythm, you'll really enjoy weaving. The weaving then becomes relaxing, sometimes even meditative, and your fabric will be more balanced, neat, and even.

Although easy to make, and therefore accessible to beginners, plain weave is certainly the structure on which you'll spend the most time. For while it's easy enough to go over and under a thread, which in itself is no great feat, it is precisely in this simplicity of structure that the difficulty of weaving lies, because every irregularity is noticeable. If, at a given moment, your beat is a little less or a little more forceful, it is immediately obvious. With plain weave you can't hide anything, especially when you're using a normal, smooth, texture-free yarn. It is therefore essential to find a way of beating the weave in a consistent and balanced way, which takes a certain amount of time with each new project. When I start a new piece, I treat the first

2 to 4 inches as a trial period to find the right beat. Every yarn is different, every combination of warp and weft is different. Take the time to find the right motion, then the right rhythm, to maintain the same beat.

> ### Which Heddle Position: A Tip to Remember
>
> To avoid having to wonder whether I should switch the heddle to the up or down position after a break or a moment of distraction, I've given myself a rule: when it's in the up position, I always pass my shuttle from right to left, and conversely in the down position, I pass it from left to right.
>
> So, if I'm lost, I look to see where the yarn is. If it's on the right, I have to move the heddle to the up position to pass the weft thread; if it's on the left, I have to move the heddle to the down position to continue working.

Changing Yarn While Weaving

You may need to change yarns while weaving, either because your shuttle is empty or because you want to use a different color. In this case, proceed as for the first thread of your weft.

1 Open the shed and wrap the rest of your thread around the first warp thread at the bottom. Lay about ½ inch of yarn into the shed parallel to the last woven row and pull the remaining tail down under the weave.

2 Repeat for the new thread (yellow in photo). First pass the new shuttle through the shed, leaving 2 to 3 inches of yarn outside the warp. Wrap this end around the first warp thread at the bottom, tuck it into the shed, place about ½ inch next to the previous weft pick and bring the tail end out under the weave.

The small extra thickness thus created should not be visible on the finished piece.

3 At the end of the weave, use scissors to cut off these two yarn tails on the back of the weave.

Advancing and Winding the Warp

As your weaving progresses, it will come closer to the heddle, making it increasingly difficult to pass the shuttle through the shed. It will then be time to unwind a length of warp yarn from the rear warp beam and wind the fabric onto the front cloth beam.

1 Release the brake from the rear warp beam.

2 Turn the warp beam to release some unwoven warp.

3 Engage the brake again.

4 Turn the front warp beam using the handle to wind the finished fabric and advance the empty warp. You do not need to release the front brake to do this.

Wind the warp fairly often. Ideally, you should wind it about every 6 inches, rather than waiting until you can no longer pass the shuttle. This will greatly improve the evenness of your weave.

Finishing the Weave

Once you have reached the end of your warp, you can simply leave 4 inches of weft thread or tie it to the last warp thread to secure it before moving on to the next step: cutting off the woven fabric.

Removing the Woven Fabric from the Loom

There are two situations in which you'll need to cut off your woven fabric while it is still on the loom.

Using scissors to cut the woven item from the loom when completed, having finished the edge with a hemstitch.

When the Warp Is Finished

At some point, you will reach the end of your warp and will need to remove your weaving from the loom. Here is the easiest way to do it.

1 Unroll a little warp to give it some slack and cut the threads, either at the back rod or in front of the heddle. This will depend on the length of yarn you need (for a scarf fringe, for example).

Be Careful

Never cut across the whole row of yarn at once, as the fabric is very fragile when cut. In fact, you'll immediately see the last weft threads begin to unravel and come undone. To avoid this, cut only about 20 warp ends at a time, carry out all the following steps to secure the weave, then start again with the next 20 ends, and so on until the end of the warp.

2 Immediately tie the cut warp ends to secure the last weft picks. Make your knots with 4 or 8 strands. The fewer strands in the knots, the prettier the result, but it also takes a little longer.

3 Once all the strands from the back warp beam are tied, you can release the front brake and unwind the finished fabric by pulling it upward. Surprise! This is the emotional moment in every weaving project, when you can admire your work in its entirety for the first time!

36 - Complete Guide to Rigid Heddle Weaving

4 Untie the bow ties at the front.

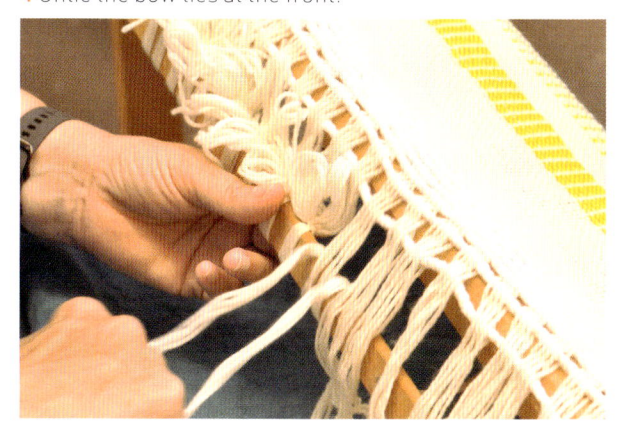

5 Remove the coarse wool used to even out the warp at the beginning.

6 Tie the front strands together, as in step 2, at the other end of the weave. Otherwise, the weft could unravel quite easily.

Before the Warp Is Finished

You can also cut some of the fabric from your warp before it is actually finished, such as when you make a sample. In this case, the idea is to not touch the threads already brought through the heddle, so as not to have to repeat this tedious step.

1 Unwind the warp to give it some slack, leaving plenty of space between the heddle and the beginning of the fabric.

2 Cut the warp in the middle between the heddle and the beginning of the fabric. As when cutting off the weave when at the end of the warp, cut the ends little by little (not all at once!).

3 Immediately tie the warp threads in front of the heddle to secure them. Tie knots that are easy to untie—they're only temporary and prevent the yarn from coming out of the slots and eyes.

4 Also tie the strands from the fabric together. Make knots with 2 or 4 threads. The fewer threads in the knot, the prettier the result, but it also takes a little longer.

5 Unwind the finished sample or fabric from the front beam and secure the warp threads with knots at this end as well.

6 Retie already warped threads temporarily secured in front of the heddle to the front rod, as if you were starting a new weave (see photo page 32, left-hand column). In this way, you can continue weaving without having to repeat a complete warping operation.

Weaving with the Rigid Heddle Loom - 37

When Things Go Wrong

My weaving teacher always used to say that to weave you have to be a bit of a MacGyver at heart. I have to admit, she's absolutely right! There is always something going wrong, a problem to be solved, yarn that breaks, etc. But it need not be dramatic; simply do not panic and know how to manage. You can repair weaving, as long as you remain calm and patient.

Tension Is Not Good

The most important thing when you're starting out is to achieve balanced tension across the warp.

If some threads are less taut than others, weaving will become an ordeal. The shed won't open properly, and there will always be yarn sagging in the middle. As well as being annoying, this problem can lead to mistakes in your fabric.

In addition, threads with poorly managed tension will tear more easily, the final fabric is likely to pucker, and the edges will be less clean.

So, before you start weaving, slide your hand over the entire layer of warp, preferably behind the heddle. This pressure will allow you to feel whether all the warp ends are evenly tensioned. At this stage, you can still tighten them without too much trouble. Simply open the bow ties on the front rod and pull a bit on the parts that are not taut enough.

If you detect the problem after you've started weaving, take a close look at the last weft picks you've made. Is the fell line of the weft straight, or do you see waves forming?

The top of the waves corresponds to threads that are too taut, the bottom to those that are too loose. If you notice this fairly quickly, you can resolve the imbalance quite easily by pulling on the threads that are a little too loose and securing them with an additional thread, on the front for example.

If, on the other hand, you find that some warp ends are getting looser and looser, and you are a ways into the project, I suggest you weight down these ends from the rear. There are two ways of doing this.

- Weight the warp ends in question with something such as a pair of scissors or a plastic egg filled with coins (a Kinder Surprise egg is my teacher Betty Briand's idea; thanks, MacGyver! See page 41).
- Put a small warp stick, chopstick, or the like under the less taut yarn to exert more tension.

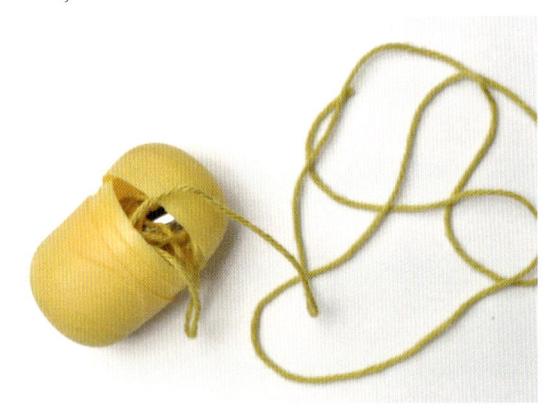

Kinder Surprise egg weighted with coins to tighten the thread

Edges Are Not Sharp

One of the most difficult things about weaving is getting clean, crisp edges. They're the bane of every weaver, always.

Edges generally tend to shrink as the work progresses. To avoid this problem, weavers **never pass the weft thread straight through the shed** before beating.

Indeed, when the shed is open, the thread placement seems perfect. But once the position of the heddle is changed, the weft thread has to follow the "over/under" movement, and if it's too short and taut, it will pull at the edge to compensate.

Here are two techniques to avoid this problem:
- make a diagonal of around 45 degrees before beating,
- make a curve or "mountain" to tamp down.

A 45-degree diagonal made with the yarn just before beating.

These two methods give the weft a little extra length, thus preventing the yarn from pulling on the edges. The 45-degree method is mainly used in standard weaving, and the mountain method in tapestry.

In addition to gradually reducing the width of the fabric, this pull-in also weakens the warp ends on the selvedges. If any tear at this point as you move forward, check that the weft picks are long enough. Carefully apply the 45-degree rule and avoid pulling in on the edges.

Another way to prevent edges from shrinking is to use a **temple**. This is a width-adjustable tool with teeth that are inserted into the weave so that the latter always stays at the same width. Remember to move it after every 4 to 6 inches of weaving. It can be very useful for fabrics that absolutely must retain their width, such as rugs or curtains. On the other hand, its very sharp teeth can themselves weaken the edges and are not suitable for delicate fabrics.

Weft Is on an Angle

You'd like your last weft pick to be straight and perpendicular to the loom, but as you are weaving, perhaps you realize that the weft you have tamped down is increasingly at an angle. To remedy this, here are two tips.

- Make sure you place your hands on the heddle symmetrically, i.e., on both sides of the weave and at an equal distance from the edge of the heddle.
- To beat, choose a spot on the loom parallel to the fabric, such as part of the front frame, and ensure that the heddle remains parallel to this mark at the end of beating.

Shed Does Not Open Properly

Sometimes the shed doesn't open properly. Check the following points.

- Do you have enough tension on the warp? Beginners are generally afraid of breaking the warp, and don't put enough tension on the yarn to ensure that the shed opens properly. In this case, add tension by turning the front brake one or two notches.
- Do you have yarn in the middle of the shed? This may be due to a problem with the tension of some warp ends; see page 38. It is also possible that you have made a mistake during warping. Check that you've warped all the slots and eyes correctly and that, for example, no slots contain two warp ends.
- Have you positioned the heddle correctly?
- Are your yarns very hairy? Not only mohair yarns, but hairy wools too, can cling together to the point where it is impossible to open the shed properly. In this situation there's no real solution, and you'll have to untangle these threads with your fingers with every weft pick, or possibly just change the warp.

Fabric Is Too Stiff or Too Loose

Normally, once you have followed the steps described above, you'll have calculated the density of your fabric according to the yarn selected, made a sample, and cut it from the loom before washing it.

If, despite all these calculations, you realize that the fabric you have made is not what you expected, that it's too stiff or too loose for your project, you have two choices:

- experiment with other weft yarns, ones either thinner or thicker, from a different fiber, etc.,
- change the warp density.

When Things Go Wrong - 39

To change the warp density on a rigid heddle loom, you will need to change the heddle.

If the fabric is too loose, use a heddle with more ends per inch. If the fabric is too tight, opt for a heddle with fewer ends per inch.

It is possible to leave the warp wound on the back rod, but unfortunately, you will have to rethread the heddle. To avoid tangling and crossing the threads while rewarping, here is a technique you can try that is used for treadle looms. Insert two warp sticks or two pieces of cardboard into the warp to separate the threads one by one so you can warp them without any problem (as shown in the photo opposite).

1 Set the heddle in the up position. Insert a warp stick or piece of cardboard wider than the loom between the top and bottom warp, behind the heddle.

2 Now move the heddle to the down position and insert a second stick into the warp opening.

3 Hold these two sticks together, with rubber bands for example, to prevent the threads from escaping.

4 Now you have separated the warp thread by thread and you can see on the warp sticks exactly the order of the threads to be warped.

5 Now carefully cut and remove the threads from the heddle and replace with a new heddle, more suitable for the desired density.

6 Thread the new heddle, alternating eyes and slots.

Yarn Breaks

One of the most frustrating things in weaving is to see a warp thread break. Unfortunately, this happens from time to time, and you need to look for the cause.

- The warp thread used is simply too fragile, unable to withstand the friction from the heddle, and the tension causes it to break.
- The yarn may have a defect where it breaks.
- You may have snagged the thread when using the shuttle.

The main thing now is not to panic, but to stay calm. This is not the end of the world, and you're not going to throw your whole project in the garbage. **A broken yarn can be repaired!** (Remember MacGyver?) My favorite technique is to replace the entire warp end.

1 Cut a new piece of yarn the same length as the original warp.

2 Remove the end of the broken length of warp from the back warp beam behind the heddle and simply let it hang down behind the loom.

3 Place the replacement thread in the heddle.

4 Pull on the broken thread to remove it from at least 1 to 1½ inches of the weft.

5 Using a needle, insert the new warp end through the 1 to 1½ inches of weft you've just opened up. Be sure to follow the same path as the warp thread being replaced.

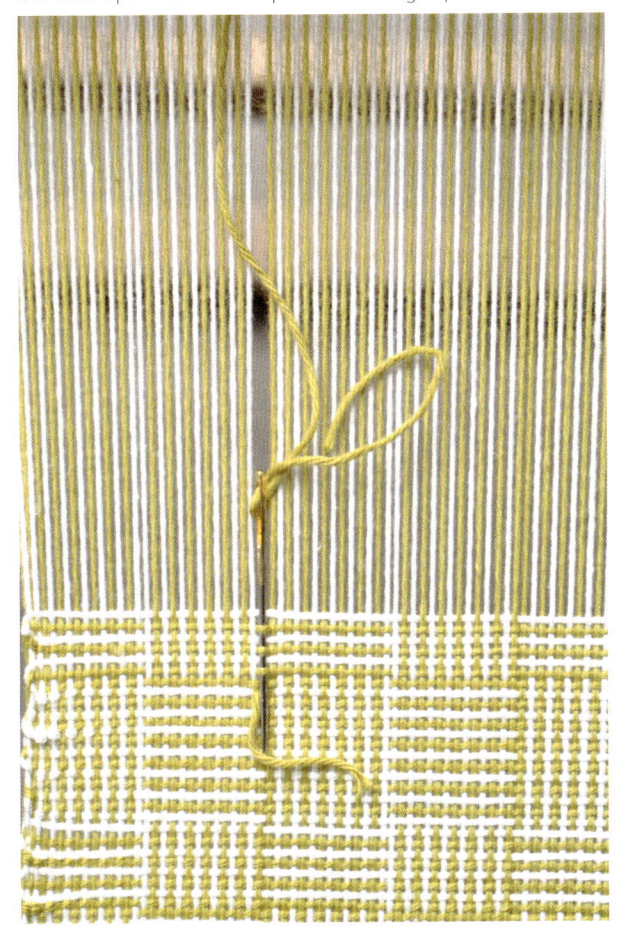

6 Wrap the end of the broken thread and the end of the new thread around a T-pin to prevent them from escaping. Insert this pin into the fabric.

7 Weight the new thread at the back of the loom to give it the same tension as the other warp ends. Be creative! I often use the plastic egg found in Kinder Surprise, but any kind of plastic egg will do. I wedge in the length of thread and insert coins to give it more heft (see page 38).

When Things Go Wrong

8 Resume weaving as if nothing had happened.

9 When you have finished the weaving project and the fabric has been cut from the loom, remove the T-pin. Using a needle, weave in the threads that were attached to it on the back side of the fabric, following the weft in one direction and then the other to secure them. Then cut off any protruding tails.

Length of Fabric Woven Is Difficult to Estimate

As you progress, you'll need to roll up the fabric, which raises two big questions: how do you know what length you have woven, and how much you still have left to do?

This can be very problematic for a project requiring exact dimensions, or if you want to make two pieces of the same size (dish towels, for example).

One way to measure is to pin a tape measure to one side of your fabric and roll it up as you weave. This way, you will always know exactly how much you have already woven.

Another option is to replace the tape measure with paper templates whose measurements match those of your finished piece. Pinned to the fabric, it can stay with it on the beam, enabling you to visualize precisely the length you still have left to weave.

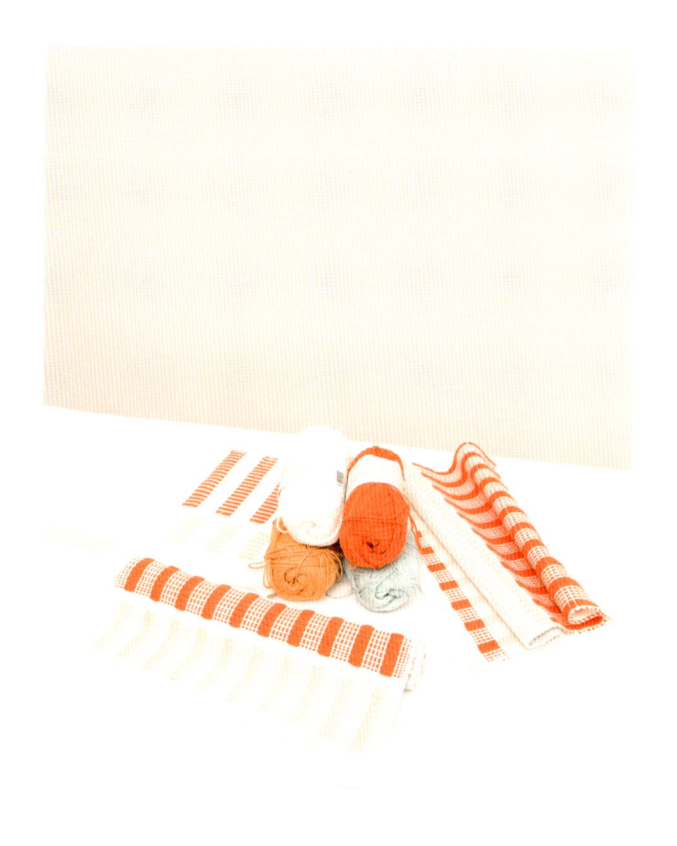

Finishing Steps

You need to consider finishing techniques right from the start of your project, rather than waiting until the weaving is completed.

While some finishes can be done right at the end of weaving without any preparation, before the fabric is cut from the loom, others must be stitched right from the first rows. Some finishes, such as fringe, must be planned back when you calculate the length of yarn needed for warping the loom.

Finishes can influence both warping and weaving, so it is best to anticipate this step to avoid later hassles.

Securing the Weave

The most important thing, when you want to remove your finished fabric or sample from the loom, is to secure the warp ends to prevent the first and last weft rows from unraveling. If you have not hemstitched across the fabric when weaving (see opposite), there are three other finishing techniques to choose from.

1 Make double overhand knots with 2 or 4 warp ends. Tie the knots tightly against the weft but make sure the weft remains straight. This is the simplest (but not necessarily the most aesthetic) way of securing the warp. It is useful when you are in a hurry and the edges of the project won't be visible in the finished piece, such as if you're planning on hems.

2 Make square knots with 2 or 4 strands, which are more aesthetically pleasing than overhand knots, but also take longer to make. These knots are a good base for finishing the edges with fringe.

3 Once you've cut the weave off the loom, run the edges through a serger. I do this for all my sewing samples and fabrics. If you don't have a serger, the zigzag stitch on a sewing machine comes close. This stitch ensures clean edges and a weave that will hold together properly.

Hemstitch

If I had to recommend one technique to learn, it would be this one, as it is not only one of my favorite finishes, but also a great way to secure the weave.

Done by hand with a needle, this stitch gives a very clean, decorative, and durable look to the project. While it is a little more time-consuming than knots, it is well worth the investment.

Note that you need to plan for this finish from the outset, as the first hemstitch is done soon after the warp is in place. The second takes place at the very end of weaving. While there are some differences between the process at the beginning and end, hemstitch is always done from right to left. But can I tell you a secret? On a rigid heddle loom, you can easily work the end hemstitch the same as the beginning one by simply turning the loom at the end of weaving.

At the Beginning of the Weave

1 With your weft yarn, leave a long tail equivalent to at least 3 times the width of the item hanging outside the warp and then weave the first 4 rows. This is the yarn you will use for sewing the hemstitch.

2 Don't beat these 4 rows too tightly, as you'll be working the hemstitch just between the heavy yarn used to even out the warp and the beginning of the weave. Take a needle and thread the long tail of weft yarn.

3 Pass the needle from right to left **under** the warp and bring the needle up just after the fourth warp end, from the back side to the front side of the weave.

4 Insert the needle again at the starting point, from right side to the wrong side of the weave.

5 Again pass the needle back under the first 4 warp ends and, instead of bringing it up after the fourth, as in step 3, insert your needle just above the last weft row. This will create an upward diagonal that will trap the 4 warp threads bordering the weave.

6 Repeat steps 3 to 5 until you have knotted the warp ends across the entire width of the weft, finishing with a knot. Each time you wrap the warp ends, pull the sewing thread tight enough to close the knots from the previous round.

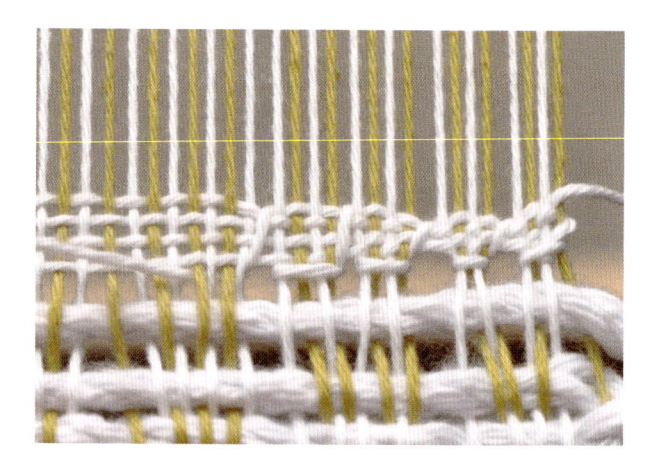

7 Once you have finished weaving, you can cut your fabric ½ inch from the knots without further concern of unraveling.

At the End of the Weave

For this finish, you must weave your last weft from left to right, leaving a tail at least equivalent to 3 times the width of the warp.

1 Insert the end of the weft thread into a needle.

2 Pass the needle from right to left under the warp, bringing up the needle just after the fourth warp end, from back to front.

3 Reinsert the needle back at the starting point, from front side to back side. Your thread now surrounds the first 4 warp ends.

4 Pass the needle back under the first 4 warp ends and bring it out just below 4 weft picks. This will create a sort of descending diagonal that will trap the 4 warp threads bordering the weave.

5 Repeat steps 2 to 4 until you've knotted the warp ends across the entire width of the weft. Each time you wrap the warp ends, pull the sewing thread tight enough to close the knots from the previous round.

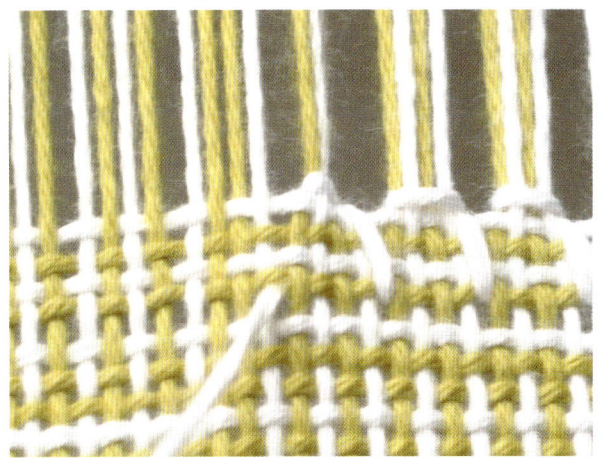

6 Once you've finished weaving, you can cut your fabric ½ inch from the knots without further concern of unraveling

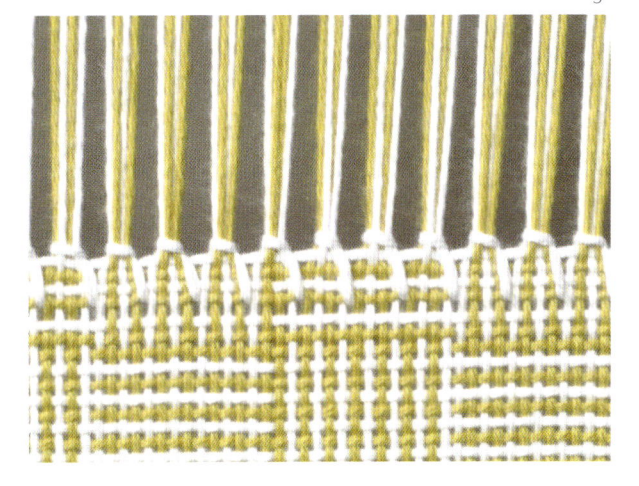

Finishing Steps - 45

> **Mnemonic Tip for the Hemstitch**
>
> The hemstitch is constructed in much the same way at the beginning and end of the weave, but as it borders the weave, it must be done:
>
> - before the first weft pick (the thread surrounds the warp before the first weft row, then moves up to be inserted between the 4th and 5th rows of the weave),
> - then, after the last weft pick (the thread wraps around the warp after the last weft row, then moves down to be inserted between the 4th and 5th previous rows of the weave).
>
> To remember where to insert the needle, I say to myself:
>
> - at the beginning of the weave: I build the floor then go up the stairs,
> - at the end of the weave: I build the ceiling then go down the stairs.

Fringe

If you need a visible decorative finish, on a scarf for example, a fringe is ideal.

However, these finishes need to be planned well in advance, right from the initial calculations, as they require an extra length of warp, as we saw on page 22.

There are several types of fringe.

- Simple fringe: After cutting your project off your loom, make square knots with the number of warp ends chosen beforehand. For a cleaner, more decorative look, each fringe should contain the same number of threads, depending on their thickness. In general, we use between 2 and 8 threads per fringe. If you like math and are a perfectionist, you can of course calculate the number of strands per fringe by dividing the number of warp ends by the number of fringe knots to be made, for greater regularity. For example, if you have 110 warp ends, you can opt for 22 fringe knots of 5 strands each (110 ÷ 5 = 22).

  Be sure to knot the threads as close as possible to the last weft to secure it, without distorting it. Try to be consistent to create a pretty edge. You can leave the fringe as is, or even the yarn out with a rotary cutter or scissors. Use a large ruler to cut all fringe to the same length.

- Twisted fringe: instead of securing the last weft with square knots, you can also make twisted fringe straight away. Determine the number of strands your fringe will contain and divide by two. Take the first half between your right thumb and index finger, and the other half with your left hand. Roll each group of threads, to the right for example, to create tension. Intertwine the right-hand and left-hand threads before tying the end with a square knot. Let go and see how nicely the fringe rolls together. Wash the piece and trim the edges of the fringe under the knots, for a cleaner look. To make things easier, you can also use a fringe twister.

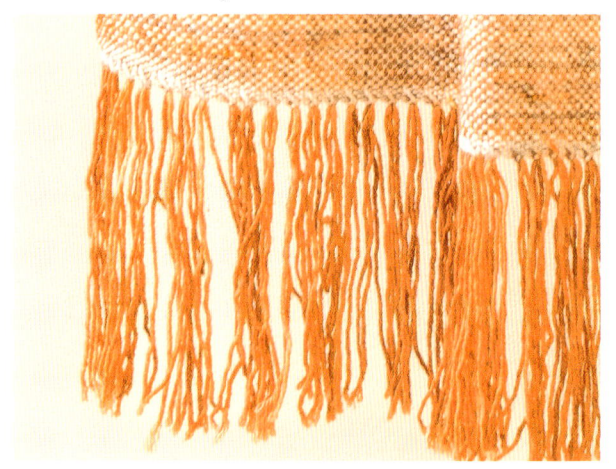

Simple fringe

Twisted fringe

Washing and Ironing

One of the most important steps for me is washing the fabric right after it is woven.

On the loom, the fabric is under constant tension and, once released, usually begins to ripple. It often looks crumpled or stiff. Washing relaxes all the fibers. Some swell, some shrink, but either way they take their final place.

Remember

You can't judge your fabric until it's been washed and dried completely!

Take the time to experience it for yourself. I assure you: a fabric can really change its look. I steam-iron all my fabrics after I've washed them, and I'm always amazed at the results. It is a magical moment for me.

Be sure to secure the warp before washing, at least with basic double knots, so it doesn't come undone during the washing.

Wash the fabric considering the type of fibers used. If the fabric is made of wool, for example, soak it in lukewarm water with a little shampoo or suitable detergent, rinse it, then dry flat. A cotton or linen fabric can easily be machine-washed and then ironed with a hot iron.

Serger

Another of my favorite finishes is sewing with the serger. I choose this method when the decorative aspect is not important, and I don't want to waste time.

For example, I don't need to do the hem stitch for a sample. I take it directly to the serger, which cuts and secures my fabric at the same time.

The same applies to all fabrics that are to be sewn or hemmed. Beautiful finishes would disappear in the seam allowances or hems. Knots or a hem stitch would also add an undesirable thickness to a hem.

The zigzag stitch on a sewing machine achieves much the same result. The advantage of the serger is that it trims off the fabric as it stitches, giving a cleaner edge.

Hems

Some projects, such as placemats or dish towels, require a simple, clean, and attractive finish.

Single Hem

This is both the most basic and the thinnest of hems.

1 Cut the fabric from your loom and secure the edges with a serger or the zigzag stitch on your sewing machine.

2 Fold inward about ½ inch, making sure the edges are straight, then pin.

3 Iron the fold to give it its final shape, and then sew with a straight stitch by machine or by hand about 3/16 inch from the edge.

I often apply this finish to my rugs, as a double hem would be too thick. However, in this case, I don't cut the edges with the serger. I tie the warp with double knots and hide the threads in the hem.

Double Hem

This is the most common hem, especially for clothing and linens. It is thicker, but also cleaner. It allows the edge of the weave to be enclosed within the hem, preventing it from becoming visible and fraying.

1 Cut the fabric from your loom and secure the edges with a serger or the zigzag stitch on your sewing machine.

2 Fold the edge inward once by ½ inch, then iron it.

3 Fold the fabric inward a second time by ½ inch and iron again. The serged or oversewn edge should now be completely hidden inside your fold.

4 Sew with a straight stitch, by machine or by hand, close to the edge of the first fold, as seen in the photo.

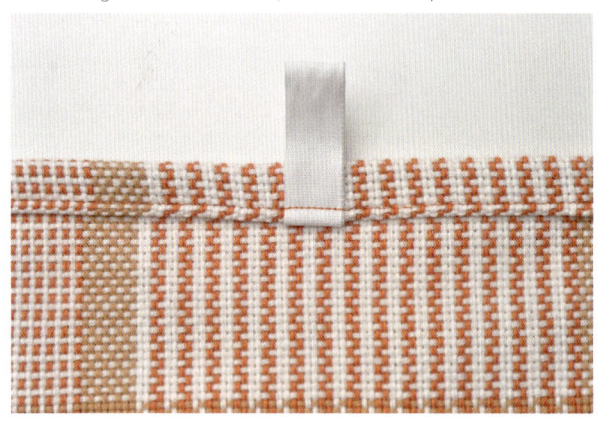

Bias Tape

Another option is to place bias tape or binding on the edges of your fabric. Like the double hem, this finish is aesthetically pleasing and traps the edge inside the fabric, avoiding any risk of fraying.

1 Pin your bias tape to the entire edge of your fabric.

2 Iron the whole thing and check that the bias tape is correctly positioned on both sides of the fabric.

3 Sew in straight stitch, by machine or by hand, close to the open edge.

Interfacing

Interfacing isn't really a finish in the true sense of the word, but since I use it so often, I thought I'd mention it.

I know that many of you dread the moment of cutting and sewing handwoven fabric, fearing that everything will unravel or fray. Although this won't necessarily happen, interfacing can alleviate your fears by reinforcing the fabric.

I generally use an interfacing that goes on the reverse side and is simply applied with an iron. Most often, I buy Vlieseline H200, easily found in a sewing supplies or fabric store.

Once you've stabilized your fabric, you can cut it with scissors without having to secure it with a serger or zigzag stitch.

Of course, interfacing is not an option for every project. It stiffens the fabric considerably and makes the reverse side unsightly. However, it is a good choice for pockets, bags, rugs, or pillows, for example.

Felting

Handwoven fabrics can also be stabilized by felting. It may sound strange, but light felting has the same effect as interfacing. It holds the fibers together, stabilizing them and making it easier to work with your fabric. It does, however, make the fabric denser and less fluid, so take time to consider the quality of fabric you want.

Of course, your weave must be made from a fiber that felts, ideally a 100% wool yarn. It is even more important to prepare for this finish in advance, as felting will **shrink your fabric** enormously. Only a sample made in advance will enable you to know exactly how much material you will lose, but you should be aware that a shrinkage of 10% to 20% is possible.

To felt a fabric, you need a combination of hot water, soap, and friction, and sometimes even a thermal shock to finish. I always do the felting by hand as the effect I am after is slight, and I want to be able to control it every moment.

1 After securing your fabric and removing it from the loom, immerse it in very hot, soapy water.

2 Twist it and move it around a lot.

3 Take it out from time to time to observe the progress.

If you wish to felt further, put the fabric in a tub of cold water for a few minutes, then put it back in very hot water, several times in a row. Thermal shock can further accelerate the process.

Once felting is complete, you can work with your fabric easily and without fear.

I use this technique for my wool pillows and cushions, and I love the effect. It can also be used for bags and pouches, and even for garments and scarves. Just remember to take shrinkage into account.

A Little Warning!
Even with preparation, felting is a game of chance. You can do your best, but it is impossible to control it completely.

Pillow design after felting

Sewing

You can work with your woven fabric just as you would with any store-bought fabric. It may seem a little frightening at first, but with time and experience, you will get used to it.

While you need to take a few precautions to avoid unpleasant surprises, nothing compares to the pleasure of having a garment or bag that you've made yourself from A to Z. Here are a few tips for a project that will last.

- As with all fabrics of this nature, it is important to secure the edges of the pieces with a serger or a zigzag stitch on the sewing machine to prevent unraveling, unless you have felted or interfaced them beforehand (see previous pages).
- Interface or felt your fabric, if the project lends itself to it or if the fabric needs reinforcement.
- Choose projects that require as little cutting as possible, so as not to weaken the fabric.

Finishing Steps - 49

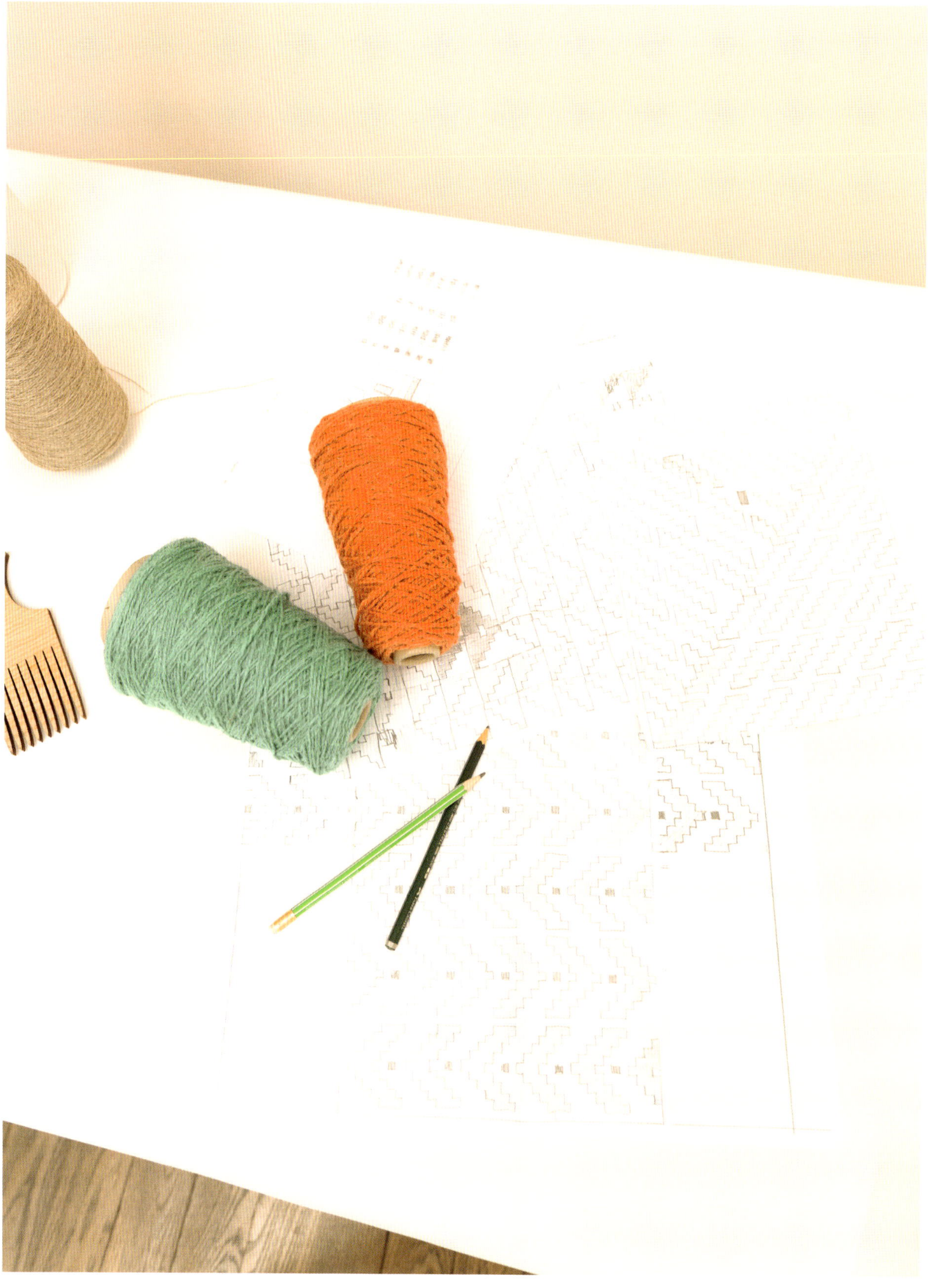

VARIOUS WEAVE STRUCTURES AND STITCHES

Here you will find a variety of techniques to enrich your weaving repertoire.

While the rigid heddle loom is undeniably a machine for making plain weave, its possibilities extend far beyond this type of fabric, provided you use a few extra tools: your fingers, a pick-up stick, or a second heddle.

But is it really that serious? Does plain weave have to be boring and be left behind as quickly as possible? I don't think so.

I suggest you discover plain weave in all its forms, and then explore the other possibilities offered by the rigid heddle loom when you add a few accessories.

Plain Weave and Variations

Contrary to popular belief, the simple plain weave is not so simple! It offers so many variations and possibilities that we could spend months experimenting!

It is also the ideal structure for highlighting the beauty of a material or color in your weaving.

> ### Which Yarn to Choose
>
> For patterned weaves, I recommend using a solid color, untextured wool, so that the design stands out. For a simple plain weave, you can opt for a more original material that will take center stage. The plain weave will serve as your "canvas," so play with colors and textures.

Playing with Yarn Choice

Colors

The first way to make a plain weave more interesting is to play with colors. Here are a few ideas to explore.

Multicolor Yarns

The easiest way to play with colors is to use a yarn that does it for you. I like to work with hand-dyed yarns, especially variegated or speckled. The results are always spectacular and quite unpredictable. I love this "surprise" aspect! If, as happens to me regularly, you have fallen for some hand-dyed balls at a fair or on the Internet, and they're now sitting alone in your stockpile and you don't know what to do with them, weave them! With just two balls of sock yarn, you can create a unique scarf. The color mixes and random patterns will leave you speechless, I guarantee it!

Different Colors or Textures in Warp and Weft

With this configuration, you can easily obtain a more original and nuanced fabric. For example, you will get pretty reflections by opting for a shiny yarn for the weft and a matte yarn, but of the same hue, for the warp. Explore the different combinations available to you and compare their effects, without complicating the weaving.

Stripes

By alternating different color warp yarns, you can create **vertical stripes** quite easily, either regular or irregular, in two or more colors.

By using several colors in the weft, you can create **horizontal stripes**. Whether the stripes are regular or irregular, the most important thing to determine is the number of colors, and therefore shuttles, to prepare, because you'll need to change the thread as you weave.

Checks

If you make a warp with stripes and use the same colors to make stripes in the weft, you'll get a checked fabric. For example, you could use this color sequence for the warp and weft: 2 white, 16 blue, 16 green, 2 white, 16 blue, 16 green, 2 white.

Textures

The second way to enhance your plain weave is to explore different textures.

Handspun Wools

Handspinning always results in a more interesting yarn. It has character and often features irregularities, large or small, perfect for enlivening a plain weave and giving it a surface you want to touch. For an even greater effect, use Artyarns brand yarns that are expressly spun with lots of texture and often several types of fibers.

Yarns with Different Textures or Materials

Alternating smooth and bouclé yarn, or even mohair, will give you an original fabric that will give more substance to your weave. While warp yarns have their limitations (see page 19), you can be more creative with weft yarns.

Plain Weave and Variations - 53

Combining Smooth and Rustic Yarns

By using natural linen and linen with small irregularities, or by using the former with a linen in a different thickness, you can create a lively and interesting surface.

Unusual Yarns

Metal yarn, paper, strips of fabric, plant materials—anything is a possibility for the weft! Of course, this depends on your project and the intended use of your weaving. Make it a real work of art!

Color Effects

In weaving, techniques allow you to create a pattern simply by alternating two colors of yarn in a certain pattern.

Houndstooth

Despite its complicated appearance, the structure of this pattern is very easy to create. It involves alternating 2 colors in warp and weft, creating regular, identical sequences of stripes.

For example, warp the loom alternating 2 blue threads and 2 white threads and weave in the same sequence, with 2 blue weft picks and 2 white weft picks. You'll get the famous houndstooth pattern.

By changing the sequence in which the blue and white yarns are placed in the warp and weft, you will discover a multitude of other patterns.

Recommendations

- Use two very distinct colors.
- Be careful when beating. If you tamp down too much, as is often done in the beginning, you won't see the pattern. It is particularly important here that the number of rows per inch matches your warp density. For example, with a density of 10 ends per inch, you'll need to beat so as to also have 10 weft rows per inch. Otherwise, the houndstooth will be completely flattened.
- You can, of course, use several different patterns in the same piece. For example, warp your loom in this sequence:
    - 1 white thread and 1 blue thread over 4 inches,
    - then 2 white threads and 2 blue threads over 4 inches,
    - finally, 4 white threads and 4 blue threads over 4 inches.
- If necessary, separate these sequences of stripes with 2 threads of a third color to clearly distinguish the different parts. Then weave the same sequences. This will give you a nice sampling of several possible patterns. I often do this exercise with my students to help them understand all the possibilities of this technique.

1 Warp your loom alternating 2 white and 2 blue threads for the entire width. Note that, to do this, you must place the white yarn in one slot and the blue yarn in the next, as at first you have 2 threads in each slot. Both colors of yarn are going to cross behind the heddle; don't pay any attention to this—it doesn't matter.

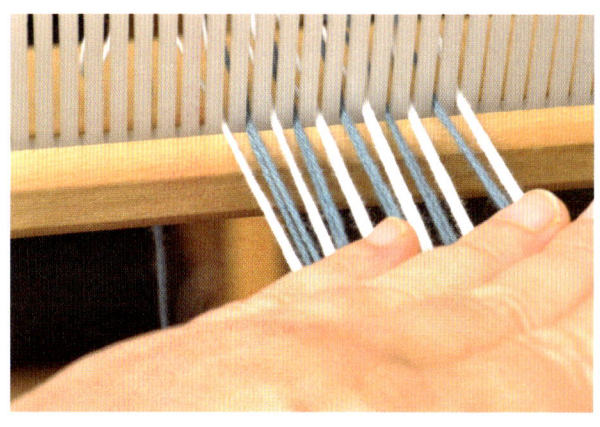

2 Prepare one shuttle with the white yarn and another with the blue.

3 Now consistently weave 2 rows in white and 2 rows in blue. At the end of each row, to ensure clean edges, always wrap the threads in the same way. Bring the woven thread over or under the previous thread. After 4 to 8 rows, you'll see the pattern appear.

Warning

Don't beat too forcefully. If you tamp down too hard, the pattern will be completely flattened and won't stand out (see explanations opposite).

4 After weaving at least 4 to 6 inches, test other patterns by trying the following combinations:
- 4 inches with white thread only,
- 4 inches with blue thread only,
- 4 inches alternating 1 row in blue and 1 row in white,
- 4 rows in white and 4 rows in blue,
- invent another pattern that covers at least 2 to 4 inches.

Plain Weave and Variations

Log Cabin

The log cabin is an intriguing motif that is a little different from the other color effect patterns in this section.

As in the other patterns, the loom must be warped by alternating the light and dark colors in regular, identical intervals.

Look at the log cabin pattern as two blocks, A and B:

- A = alternate 1 light thread/1 dark thread,
- B = alternate 1 dark thread/1 light thread.

So, when switching between the two blocks, you have to warp/weave two dark yarns or two light yarns, before returning to the regular alternation. The entire pattern is based on this nuance. And that's it, the mystery of the log cabin has been solved!

Clasped Weft

Contrary to popular belief, clasped weft is a simple technique, but the result is quite spectacular. Two wefts are used simultaneously, joined in the shed before beating with the heddle. Generally, one wool is loaded on a shuttle and the other remains in a ball.

Recommendations

- When using this technique, be careful with the edges, as they tend to shrink considerably.
- The important thing is that the two weft threads be very distinct, so that the effect really stands out.
- Patterns should be geometric, either with straight lines, or (my preference) random, organic patterns.

1 Place the first weft thread on a shuttle and leave the second on the left side of your loom in a ball.

2 Open the shed by moving the heddle to the up position. Pass the shuttle from right to left and pull it out to the left.

3 Wrap the shuttle around the yarn from the ball and reinsert it in the same shed, from left to right.

4 Do not change the position of the heddle and pull the yarn from the ball at the same time as the yarn from the shuttle to the right, to place them according to the desired pattern. Adjust the yarn placement and the join as needed.

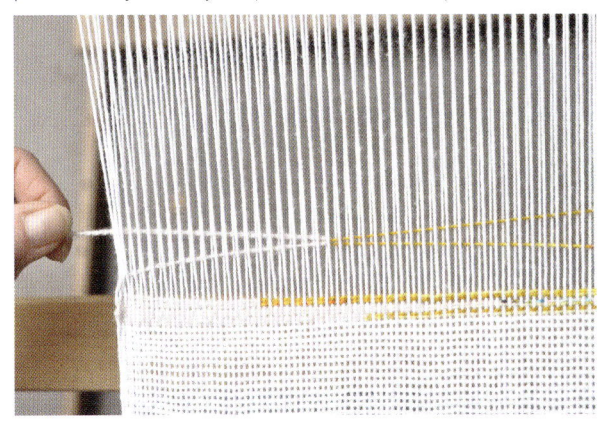

5 Beat and change heddle position.

6 Reinsert the shuttle from right to left and repeat steps 3 and 4 until the weave is complete.

Playing with Weave Effects

Spaced Warp and Weft or Different Densities in Warp and Weft

A very simple way to create effects in the weave is to leave gaps in the warp and/or weft.

Simply skip some slots when warping and continue with the same yarn an inch or so further on. You can then continue weaving as usual. In the warp spaces, there will be long floats.

You can also leave gaps when weaving the weft to create square open spaces. The easiest way to do this is to insert spacers in the places you want to leave empty, i.e., pieces of cardboard the size of the holes you want to create. By inserting them as you weave, you'll be able to beat more easily and your holes will be more even.

You can also warp the loom with yarns of different thicknesses to create a changing density.

For even greater ease, you can use a variable-dent reed. Fairly new, it is a rigid heddle with removable sections that allows for a variation in density in a single pass. The same yarn is used here but is spaced differently across the weft.

Plain Weave and Variations - 57

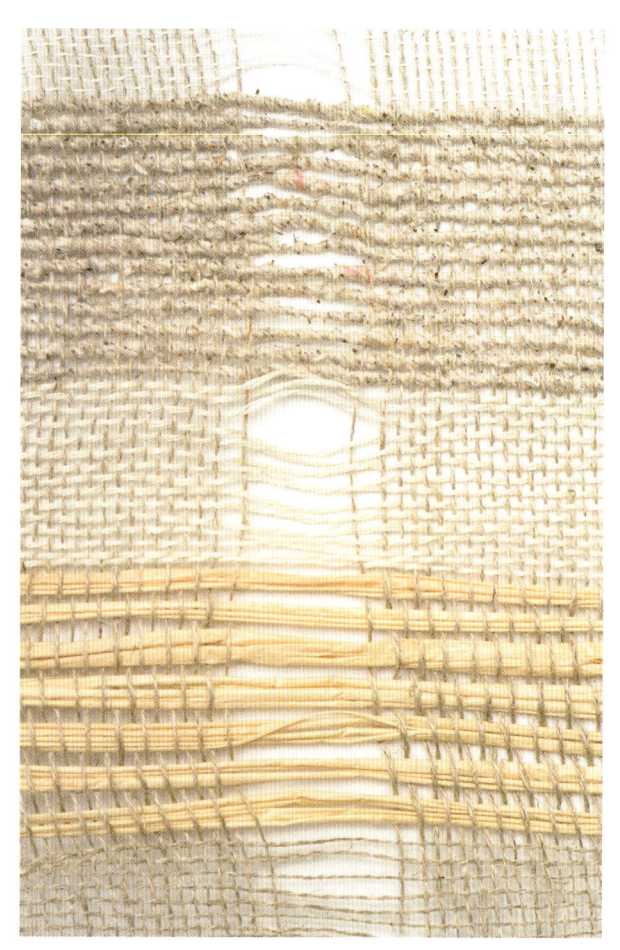

This weave is made from linen, cotton, and raffia.

Predominant Weft or Warp

Plain weave is generally a "balanced" structure, meaning you can see the warp as much as the weft when looking at the weaving. But there are also "unbalanced" variations, which allow the weaver to hide the warp (weft dominant) or the weft (warp dominant).

These fabrics are often much thicker and stiffer than conventional plain weave and, unfortunately, the density calculations seen in Part 1 don't apply here. It is therefore necessary to make a sample.

Weft Dominant

In these weaves, only the weft is visible. This is a time-consuming technique, which requires:

- much more beating than with a balanced plain weave,
- spreading the warp ends far enough apart to cover them completely.

Choose your warp carefully for these fabrics: it must be stronger than one used for a simple plain weave to withstand rigorous tamping down of the weft. It is best to use a smooth, strong warp that's thinner than the weft. As it will be covered, it doesn't play an aesthetic role.

As the warp is invisible, the design of your piece is based solely on the sequence of colors and patterns in the weft.

There are two subcategories in a weft-dominant weave.

- Tapestry: This is the only weaving variant that allows you to create nonrepetitive patterns across the width of the fabric. The special feature of tapestry is that the wefts don't run from one side of the weave to the other. On the contrary, you create your design freely, bit by bit, following a pattern developed beforehand. Rather than shuttles, small spools of different colors are used.

  In general, to follow the design, you can either attach it behind the warp, or copy it with a felt-tip pen directly onto the warp. This method allows you to create organic as well as geometric shapes.

Warp Dominant

In these fabrics, all you see is the warp. Its density is so compact that it completely covers the weft. The entire design comes through warping, which must be planned in advance. Usually, for the weft, a row of thick yarn alternates with a row of thinner yarn. This technique is often used for rugs, belts, straps, and bands.

For this technique, you need to:

- beat much more firmly than for classic plain weave,
- warp the loom very tightly, to cover the weft completely.

Tapestry weaving

- Predominantly repetitive weaving: This is basically creating a plain weave. You push your shuttle from side to side to create repetitive patterns across the width of the fabric. With no tools other than your heddle, you create lines, columns, dots, and so on. If you opt to use one or two pick-up sticks or two heddles, the designs can become more complex. One of my favorite techniques in this variation is krokbragd, a Norwegian technique described on page 92.

Krokbragd

Focus on the Japanese Saori Technique

Here is the last variation on the plain weave, one of my favorites: Saori. This fairly recent Japanese weaving technique was invented by Misao Jo in 1957. The artist felt bad that classic weaving, which is extremely technical, was accessible only to a small group of insiders, and above all, wanted weaving to be more creative.

> ### The Four "Laws" of Saori Weaving
> In Japanese, *sa* means zen and *ori*, weaving. This technique has four main principles.
> 1. Consider the differences between machines and human beings.
> 2. Be bold and try out new things.
> 3. Look at the world with shining eyes.
> 4. Be inspired by others in a group.

Unlike traditional weaving, which is highly structured, Saori is a kind of "non-technique." No patterns, no rules, no diagrams to follow. Instead, it encourages the weaver to play, experiment, have fun, explore, and mix different materials without fear or intention. It is a form of weaving that everyone can do! In fact, the less you know about weaving, the better, because it is easier to let go and explore. Saori is built on the idea that all human beings are creative and should be able to freely express this creativity in a personal way, without being bound by rules or rigid patterns.

The fact that Saori fabrics are more random, free, and sometimes even a little "wild," doesn't necessarily appeal to everyone. In Japan, these fabrics are often used to sew clothes, but I must confess that this is not my cup of tea. I love using it to create pillows, scarves, bags, pictures, and wall hangings. Very often, I take up Saori weaving after a long period of classic weaving, when I don't feel like counting all the time, but when I want to have fun.

Saori technique

To begin with, Saori is simply a canvas, nothing more; there is nothing difficult to learn or prepare. The key lies in the variety of materials you add as you go along, whatever you can get your hands on. Use all kinds of wool of course (handspun, in particular, is perfect), but also fabric scraps, plants, paper, metallic threads, wires, etc. Let your imagination run wild!

In general, we work Saori on a basic warp, light or dark, and weave in weft by adding materials in rows, entire rows or not, depending on the desired effect. Position the materials in the shed where you want them, then continue weaving above them with your basic shuttle to secure them. You can pull these positioned materials outward, make little balls, let them come out on the sides, etc. There really are no rules.

For me, it is the perfect technique for a stress-free start to weaving, without the fear of making mistakes or failing to succeed, allowing you to focus on the movement of the weave and the materials, rather than on perfect edges and beating. It is a perfect fit for the rigid heddle loom, and I hope you'll try it at least once for fun.

Tips

Although there is no real method to teach, here are a few recommendations for how to enjoy weaving Saori.

- Avoid patterns and spaces that are too regular.
- Combine different materials, thicknesses, and textures.
- Don't always beat your weft with the same force to accentuate the irregular effect.
- Use scraps and salvaged materials.
- Use the clasped weft technique.
- Incorporate bits of tapestry.
- Leave holes or gaps.
- When warping directly, skip a few slots to create effects.
- Let parts of the weft come out the sides.
- Use rya knots (see page 72).
- Weave hand-spun yarns.

Saori technique

Saori technique

Focus on the Japanese Saori Technique - 61

Other Types of Structures

While the rigid heddle loom is designed for plain weave, using some different tools allows you to change up the fun and diversify your creations. Here are a few techniques to help you discover all the possibilities available to you.

Finger-Controlled Techniques

To be able to do more than just weave plain weave and expand your stitch range, you need at least one more tool: your fingers.

The techniques described in this chapter are not achieved by pushing the shuttle back and forth across the weave. They are carried out either thread by thread, or section by section, with your fingertips. This is one way to create all kinds of openwork or textured stitches.

As you may have guessed, these techniques are rather slow and time-consuming. So arm yourself with a little patience and explore the various possibilities of what you can create with these techniques.

Openwork and Medallions

Leno

Leno is a technique used to create symmetrical, square openwork sections by twisting several warp ends together, either with the shuttle or with a pick-up stick, before inserting the weft. You can vary the number of ends to twist, depending on the desired effect.

Recommendations

- Leno is generally worked with the heddle in the up position.
- If you're right-handed, work the leno row preferably from right to left.
- You can either use your shuttle directly or a pick-up stick.
- Work with slightly less tension on the warp than usual.

1 Set the heddle in the **up** position. The outermost thread should be a top thread. Using the fingers of your left hand, push the first upper thread slightly to the left.

2 With your right hand, insert the pick-up stick under the first lower thread.

3 Pass this warp end over the pick-up stick and let the first top thread go and it will slide under the pick-up stick.

4 You have now twisted the first two warp threads together.

5 Continue in this way along the length of your warp. Always pass the bottom thread over the pick-up stick and the top thread underneath.

6 Once you've reached the end of the warp, turn the pick-up stick on its edge to leave more space between the top and bottom threads.

7 Then pass the shuttle through the shed under the pick-up stick.

Other Types of Structures - 63

8 Tamp down the weft using a hair comb if necessary.

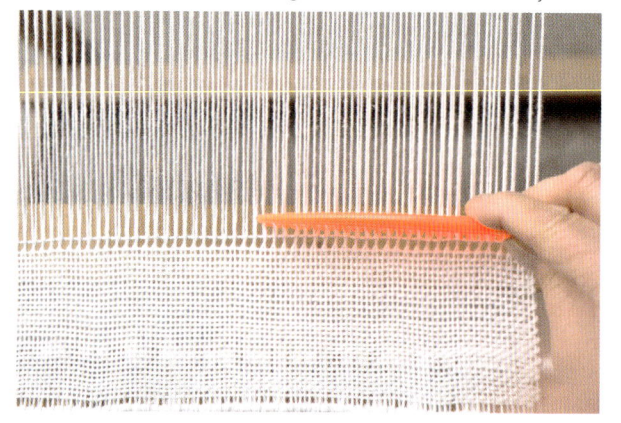

9 Move the heddle to the down position and simply pass the weft from left to right. You'll see that a second openwork row is created automatically, as the threads are still twisted.

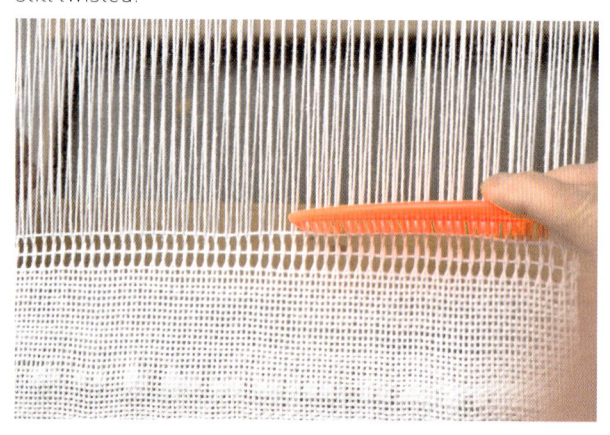

10 You can continue with a new leno row or weave an inch or so of plain weave.

Here are a few examples of leno.

Leno 1/1: Twist 2 warp ends together.

Leno 2/2: twist 4 warp ends together.

64 - Complete Guide to Rigid Heddle Weaving

Asymmetrical leno: Weave openwork over only part of the width.

Brooks Bouquet

A second technique for creating openwork fabrics is brooks bouquet. This bouquet resembles a 4-pane window and, like leno, focuses on two rows: one with openwork stitches and one with simple weaving.

The technique consists of wrapping several warp ends with your weft to create a kind of knot. You are free to choose the number of threads to wrap.

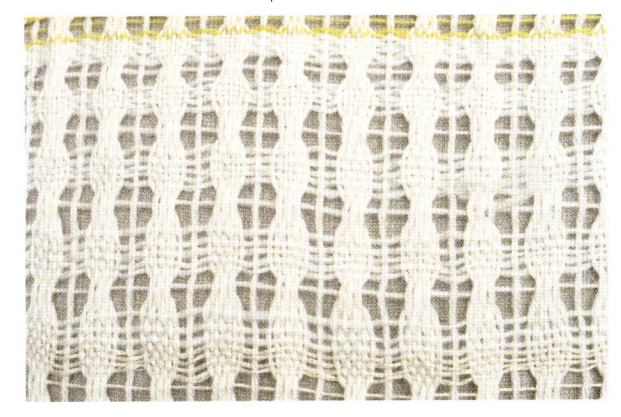

Recommendations

- Bouquets are generally worked with the heddle in the up position.
- Work the bouquet row preferably from right to left if you are right-handed.

1 Set the heddle in the **up** position..

2 Insert the shuttle into the shed, under the first 4 top warp ends, from right to left. Bring your shuttle out to the front of the weave after these 4 threads.

Other Types of Structures - 65

3 Reinsert your shuttle into the shed at the same point as in step 2, just before the first of the 4 warp ends, go under those four and under the next four as well and bring it up.

4 You have now wrapped your weft around the first 4 threads and passed under the next four.

5 Pull the weft thread to tie the first 4 warp ends together as tightly as possible.

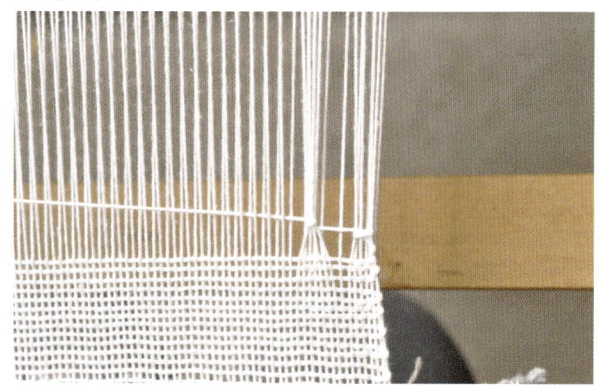

6 Reinsert your shuttle to the right of the second group of 4 threads and bring it up 8 threads further. This wraps around the second set of 4 warp threads you just passed under in step 4. Pull tightly on the weft to hold them together.

7 Repeat steps 5 and 6 all along your warp. Once the row is finished, move the heddle to the down position and simply pass your shuttle from left to right: a second openwork row is created automatically. At this stage, make sure you don't tamp down too firmly, so that the openwork in the first and second rows are the same size.

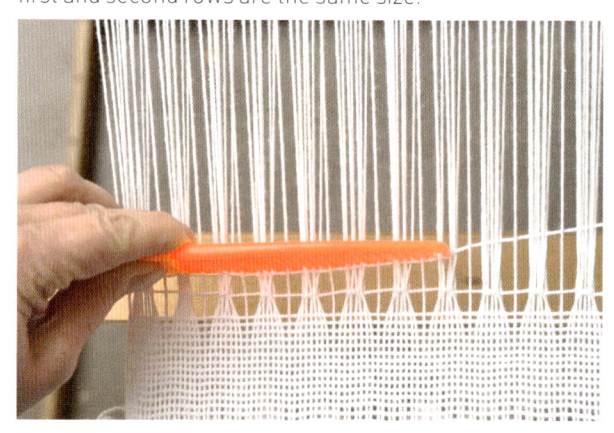

8 You can continue with the next row of bouquets or weave a few rows of plain weave first.

Danish Medallions

With this technique, you group together several sections of warp and weft and surround them with a contrasting thread to create a kind of medallion. Medallions can be more or less open, depending on how you work them. To make Danish medallions, you will need a crochet hook and two shuttles: the first containing the base yarn and the second the outline yarn.

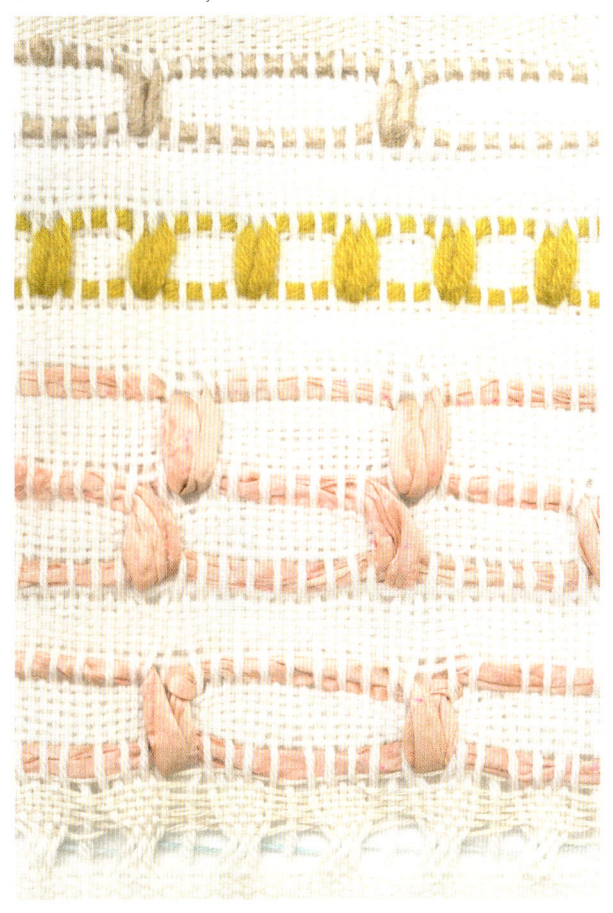

Recommendations

- Medallions are generally made with the outline yarn either thicker than the warp and weft threads, or in a contrasting color.
- The basic fabric is usually a simple plain weave, embellished with the medallions.
- You can create variations by playing with the tension exerted to trap the threads together. You can change the number of threads you include in the medallions, either within the same row or alternating from one row to the next. And, of course, don't hesitate to use several threads to change the look of the medallion.

1 The pattern begins by weaving the bottom of the medallion. Pass the shuttle containing the contrasting/thick thread from **left to right**. Set this thread aside for the moment.

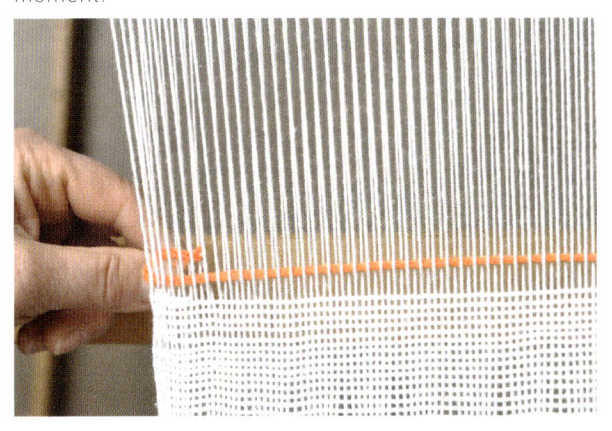

2 Using the base yarn, weave simple plain weave rows up to the height of your medallion. Finish with a row running from left to right, with the heddle in the down position.

Other Types of Structures - 67

3 You will now form the medallion. Move the heddle to the up position and insert the outline yarn set aside after step 1 into the shed.

4 Insert the shuttle under a few warp ends. These threads will be the width of your medallion; choose them according to the desired effect. Here, the medallion is 5 threads wide. Then bring out the shuttle.

5 Insert the crochet hook below the bottom border thread, next to the fifth warp thread, in line with where you pulled out the shuttle a few rows above.

6 Pass the hook behind the rows of fabric and grab the upper border thread.

7 Using the hook, bring the loop of yarn from the top edge down and out to the front of the weave.

8 Pass the shuttle containing the outline thread through the loop and pull it a little to close the loop and create a kind of knot.

9 Insert the shuttle back into the shed under the warp threads that will represent the width of the next medallion. Here, the medallions are 5 warp ends wide. Pull it out to the front as in step 4 and pick up your crochet hook to pull a new loop of contrasting yarn down and out to the front as in step 7.

10 Repeat steps 4 to 9 across the entire width of the plain weave. Once you've reached the last medallion, stop at step 4 and cut the thread, leaving a long tail.

11 To finish the last medallion on the left-hand edge of the plain weave, insert your hook between the last two warp threads below the border thread at the bottom and catch the end of the thread to bring it out to the front of the plain weave. Pull it upward and insert it into the open shed for about ½ inch to secure it. Trim the thread if it is too long.

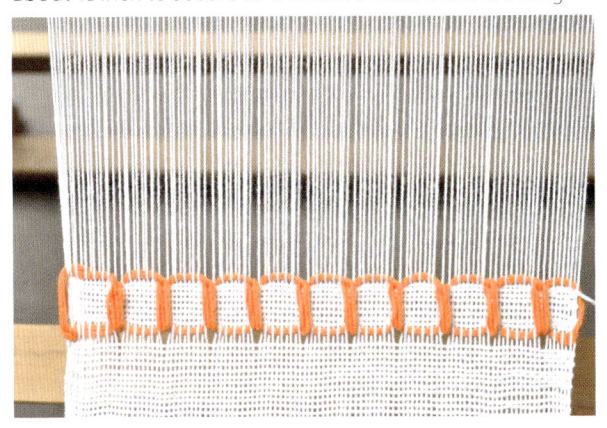

Textured Stitches

Soumak Stitch

Soumak stitch is a technique generally used to make rugs. It adds a lovely texture to your weave and is fairly easy to do. It involves wrapping one or more warp threads with the shuttle thread in a circular motion. It consists of two rows (back and forth), and the result is reminiscent of a herringbone or knitted stitch.

Recommendations

- Soumak stitch is generally worked with the heddle in neutral position.
- Choose a thicker weft than the warp to cover it completely.
- You're free to choose how many threads you want to work this stitch on, and how many you want to wrap. In patterns, the numbers are often given with a ratio of 3:1, indicating that you should go 3 warp threads further and wrap the fourth with the weft thread.
- You absolutely must work two rows of plain weave after working the soumak back and forth in order to stabilize it. The soumak stitch alone cannot create a stable fabric.

1 Weave an inch or so of plain weave with your base thread. Prepare a shuttle with the larger thread for the soumak stitch.

2 With the heddle in the up position, hide the beginning of the soumak thread, as usual, by inserting it into the shed over about ½ inch and pulling the tail out toward the back of the fabric.

3 Move the heddle to the **neutral position**.

4 Work the **1st row.** Work from right to left with a 3:1 ratio.

- Take the shuttle and pass it over the first 4 warp threads to the left.

- After the 4th warp end, pass the shuttle back into the shed and bring it back out to the front 1 thread to the right.

- Move the shuttle to the left and count another 4 warp ends after the one described in the previous step, then insert the shuttle into the shed. Pass the shuttle back and bring it up again 1 thread to the right.
- Continue this circular movement to the end of the warp to reveal a soumak strand inclined to the left.

5 Make the **2nd row.** Work from left to right.

- Take the shuttle and pass it over the first 4 warp threads to the right.

- After the 4th warp end, pass the shuttle into the shed and bring it back out to the front 1 thread to the left.

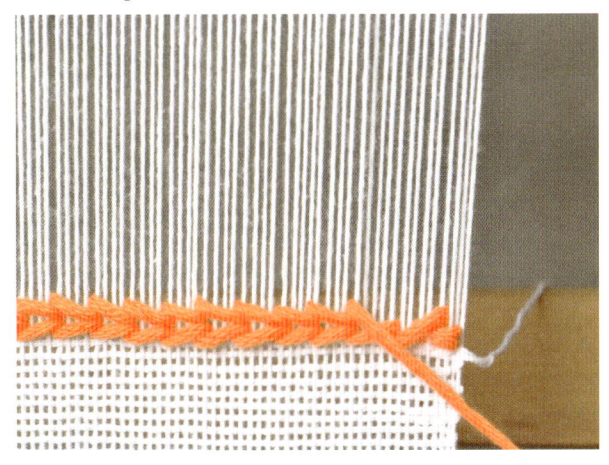

- Go to the right with the shuttle and count another 4 warp threads after the one circled in the previous step, then insert the shuttle into the shed. Pass the shuttle back 1 thread to the left and pull it out again.
- Continue this circular movement to the end of the warp to see a second soumak strand appear, this time inclined to the right. The two strands now form a V.

6 Work at least two rows of plain weave to stabilize the fabric before starting another soumak stitch.

Other Types of Structures - 71

Rya Knots

Rya knots are used to make the traditional knotted carpets you are probably familiar with. Precut yarn ends are tied around the warp to create a kind of fringe on the top of the rug.

Recommendations

- Rya knots are generally worked with the heddle in neutral position.
- I always make rya knots with precut yarn strands, but you can also do this technique with a continuous yarn that is cut as you go.
- You absolutely must make two rows of plain weave after one row of rya knots to stabilize the fabric. Rya knots alone will not produce a stable fabric.
- You can adjust the length of the threads by cutting them after stabilizing the row of rya knots with the plain weave or at the very end of the work.
- Beat firmly to stabilize the fabric.

1 Weave an inch or so of plain weave with your base yarn.

2 Cut several pieces of yarn to the same length. Make sure they are at least 1½ to 2 inches long (any shorter will be difficult to knot). If necessary, you can always shorten them at the end of weaving.

3 Set heddle in the neutral position.

4 Position the center of one of the precut yarns over 2 warp threads.

5 Pass the right-hand end of the thread between the 2 warp threads, so that it comes up on the front side of the weave.

6 Do the same with the left end, so that both strands emerge at the front of the weave between the 2 warp ends.

7 Hold the two thread ends together and pull them down against the rows of plain weave. Don't pull too hard so as not to distort the warp, but still gently close the rya knot so that it holds.

8 Continue in the same way all along the warp, always tying the knot over 2 warp ends. Weave at least 2 plain weave rows before starting a new rya row to stabilize it.

9 At the end of weaving, you can take your scissors and shorten the rya knots.

Loops

Loops are another original and easy way to add texture to your weaving. You can work them over a whole row or just a given area. Have fun!

Recommendations

- Loops can be worked with the heddle in either the up or down position.
- As with rya and soumak knots, loops alone do not create a stable fabric. You absolutely must work a row of plain weave after a row of loops to give the weave stability.
- You'll need a straight knitting needle or another tool of comparable shape.

1 Work an inch or so of plain weave with your base yarn.

2 Move the heddle to the up position. Pass the shuttle with the loop yarn from right to left. At the end of the row, leave plenty of yarn loose outside the loop shuttle. Leave the heddle in the same position.

Other Types of Structures - 73

3 Work from right to left. Pull a first loop of the weft with your fingers, bringing it to the front of the weave between the first two warp ends. Place this loop on the knitting needle.

4 Continue in this way, passing the loops up between the warp ends to the front and placing them on the knitting needle as you go. You can also use the needle directly to catch the loops between the warp threads, instead of picking them up with your fingers.

5 Place the heddle in the down position, leave the needle in place, and work a row of plain weave with the weft yarn to stabilize the loops. I usually use the same yarn for this row as for the loops.

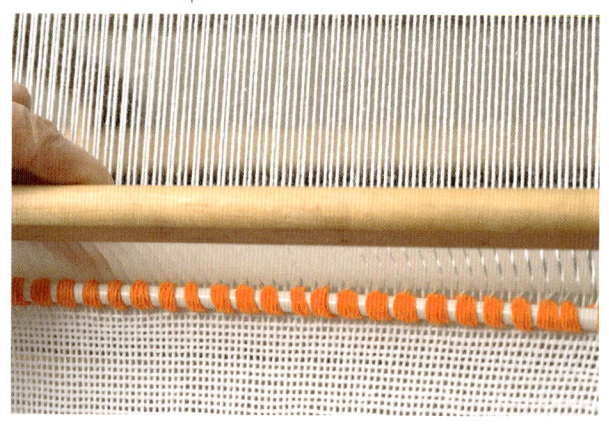

6 Remove the knitting needle. The loops are stabilized.

Weaving with a Pick-Up Stick

The pick-up stick is a flat wooden stick with at least one pointed end (see page 13). This tool allows you to pick up threads and considerably extend the range of techniques possible on a rigid heddle loom.

While the techniques for embellishing the fabric described up to now require the manipulation of each thread, the pick-up stick technique is far less time-consuming. With this tool, you can select **several warp threads at the same time** and, above all, **keep this choice** throughout the weaving process to create patterns, making the work quick and enjoyable.

This technique is possible because of the heddle's ingenious construction and the distribution of the yarn in its slots and eyes. As we have seen on page 34, the eye threads are the "active" threads, meaning they are the ones raised or lowered each time the heddle is manipulated. When the heddle is in the up position, the eye threads are at the top; in the down position the eye threads are at the bottom.

Slot threads, on the other hand, are "inactive" and always remain horizontal, but can move freely within the slot. This means they can be easily manipulated to create something other than a simple plain weave.

It is very important to understand how the loom works to know why the heddle must always be in the down position to catch the pattern threads with the pick-up stick. When the eye threads are in the down position, the slot strands are higher up and therefore more accessible.

Patterns designed with a pick-up stick rely on the creation of **floats**. Floats are threads that **pass over several warp and/or weft threads** at the same time. This technique differs from plain weave, in which each thread passes in turn under and over a single other thread. These regular floats create new patterns depending on where they are positioned, the number of threads involved, the rows in between, etc. You can even combine warp and weft floats to extend the range of possibilities.

Recommendations

There are two principles to bear in mind with these patterns.
- Floats make the fabric more fluid, but also less stable. As they always represent a risk of snagging, be careful not to make them too long.
- Weft floats on the front are warp floats on the back, and vice versa.

Some examples of floats.

Inserting the Pick-Up Stick

1 Place the heddle in the down position.

2 Insert the pick-up stick **behind the heddle** (see box below), placing the yarn over or under the stick, depending on pattern. The simplest pattern is **1 thread over** and **1 thread under**. To do this, run your pick-up stick along the entire length of the warp, placing every other warp end on the pick-up stick.

3 Once the pick-up stick has been inserted across the entire width of the warp, push it toward the back of the loom, and this will "register" the pattern.

Behind or in Front of the Heddle?

In many books and videos, the pick-up stick is first inserted in front of the heddle, then the pattern is transferred to the back with a second stick. The reason given is that it would be easier to see the threads to be caught in the front. This has always bothered me, and I find the process unnecessarily complicated. I therefore recommend inserting the pick-up stick directly behind the heddle to limit manipulations.

How to Read a Weaving Pattern

Abbreviations are common in weaving patterns. Here is an example of instructions for a pick-up stick pattern and its meaning.

Example of Instructions

Pick-up stick pattern: *1 up, 1 down*, repeat from * to * across the entire width.

Step 1: up

Step 2: pick-up stick

Step 3: down

Step 4: pick-up stick

Detailed Explanations

"Pick-up stick pattern: *1 up, 1 down*, repeat from * to * across the entire width."

To make the pattern, the first warp thread must be above the pick-up stick and the second below, and so on across the entire width, as the instructions in asterisks are to be repeated as many times as indicated.

The following steps form a pattern repeat.

"Step 1: up" means place the heddle in the up position, then pass the weft yarn through the shed.

"Step 2: pick-up stick" means place the heddle in the neutral position and place the pick-up stick just behind the heddle. Turn the pick-up stick on its edge to "stand it up" before passing the weft yarn, then lay the pick-up stick flat again.

"Step 3: down" means place the heddle in the down position and pass the weft yarn through the shed.

"Step 4: pick-up stick" means place the heddle in the neutral position and place the pick-up stick just behind the heddle. Turn the pick-up stick on its edge to "stand it up" before passing the weft yarn, then lay the pick-up stick flat again.

Repeat these steps as many times as necessary with the indicated yarn color.

Types of Floats

You can use the pick-up stick in **two different ways**, one to create weft floats and one to create warp floats.

Weft Floats (abbreviation = pick-up stick)

1 Place heddle in the **neutral position**.

2 Slide the pick-up stick directly behind the heddle.

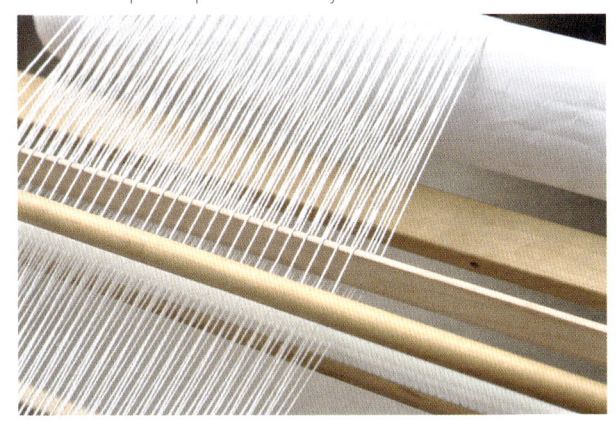

3 Turn the pick-up stick on its edge. This creates a new shed in front of the heddle, through which you can pass your weft.

4 After passing the shuttle containing the pattern yarn, push the pick-up stick back toward the rear of the loom so it is out of the way. In general, after one row with a pick-up stick, there is always at least one row without it.

Warp Floats (abbreviation = heddle up and pick-up stick)

1 Put heddle in the **up position**.

2 Place the pick-up stick directly behind the heddle, above or below the warp threads, depending on the pattern.

3 Leave the pick-up stick flat without turning it. This creates a new shed in front of the heddle, through which you can pass your pattern weft.

4 After passing the shuttle containing the pattern yarn, push the pick-up stick to the back of the loom so it is out of the way. In general, after one row with a pick-up stick, there is always at least one row without it.

Creating Floats

At first, I always had a bit of trouble visualizing what the sequences on the pick-up stick would look like when woven. There are two more things you need to understand to be able to correctly foresee what your patterns will look like.

- The threads you put on the pick-up stick are not covered by the weft yarn. It is those you leave under the pick-up stick that will be covered by floats.

- When you "register" the pattern on your pick-up stick, you only deal with the slot threads, which are then higher up than the eye threads. The latter will still be taken into account when weaving.
  - For weft floats: With the heddle in the neutral position, the eye threads are below the pick-up stick, at the same level as the slot threads, which remain below the stick. The eye threads will then also be covered by the pattern yarn.

Other Types of Structures - 77

- For warp floats: With the heddle in the up position, the eye threads are above the pick-up stick, at the same level as the threads above the stick. They will therefore not be covered by the pattern yarn.

Patterns with Weft or Warp Floats

For each pattern described below, you can either use the same weft yarn as for the rest of the weave or opt for a different one—thicker or a different color, for example, to further emphasize the pattern.

You can also insert the pick-up stick only on certain sections of the warp, rather than across its entire width, and freely vary the number of threads included in the pattern within the same row.

You can reinsert the pick-up stick with a new pattern whenever you like—after every row, every 10 rows, or not at all. Explore!

Weft Floats

Pick-up stick pattern 1: *1 up, 1 down*, repeat from * to * across the entire width of the weft.

Step 1: up

Step 2: down

Step 3: pick-up stick

Pick-up stick pattern 2: *1 up, 1 down*, repeat from * to * across the entire width of the weft.

Step 1: up

Step 2: pick-up stick

Step 3: down

Step 4: pick-up stick

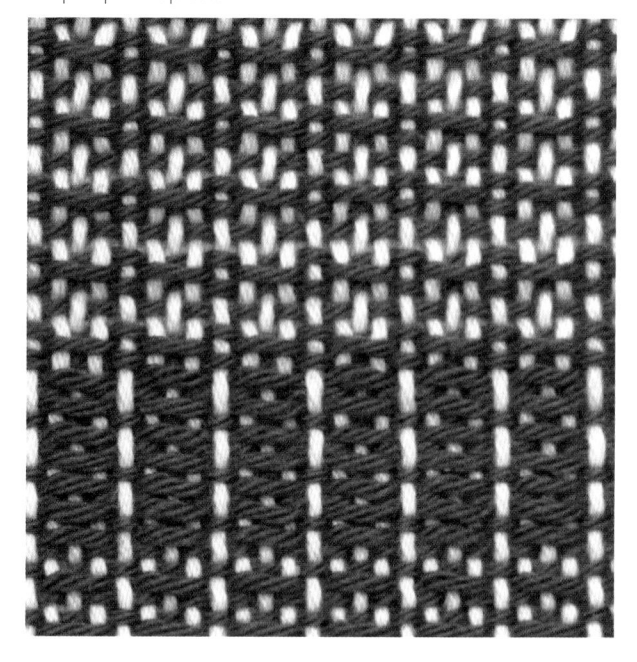

78 - Complete Guide to Rigid Heddle Weaving

Pick-up stick pattern 3: *1 up, 1 down*, repeat from * to * across the entire width of the weft.

Step 1: up
Step 2: pick-up stick
Step 3: up
Step 4: down

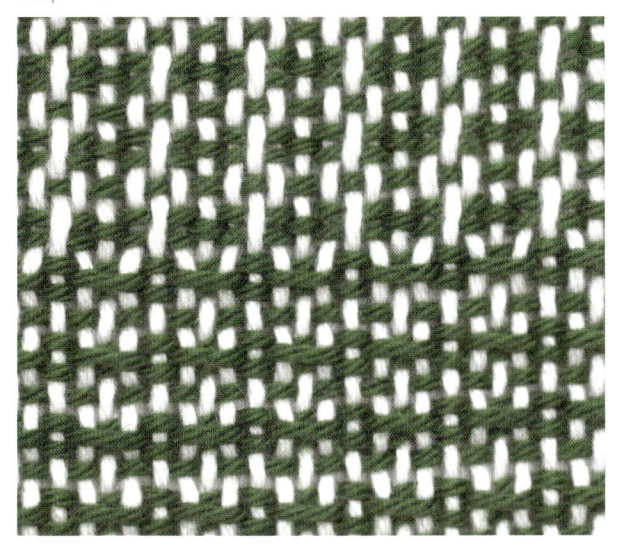

Pick-up stick pattern 4: *4 up, 1 down*, repeat from * to * across the entire width of the weft.

Step 1: up
Step 2: pick-up stick with thicker weft
Step 3: down
Step 4: pick-up stick with thicker weft
Step 5: up
Step 6: down

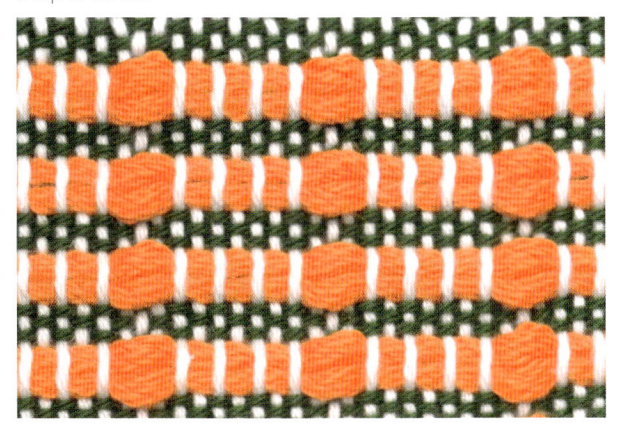

Pick-up stick pattern 5: *2 up, 2 down*, repeat from * to * across the entire width of the weft.

Step 1: up
Step 2: pick-up stick
Step 3: up
Step 4: pick-up stick
Step 5: up
Step 6: pick-up stick
Step 7: up
Step 8: down

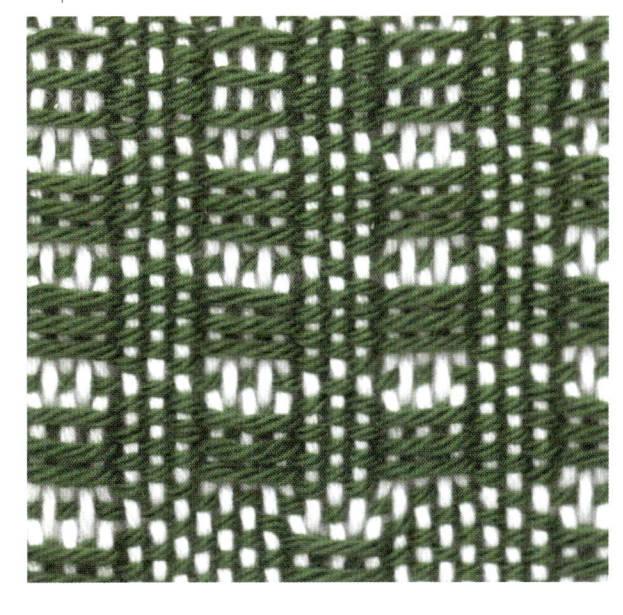

Other Types of Structures

Warp Floats

Pick-up stick pattern 1: *1 up, 1 down*, repeat from * to * across the entire width of the weft.

Step 1: down

Step 2: up and pick-up stick

Step 3: down

Step 4: up

Pick-up stick pattern 2: *5 up, 1 down*, repeat from * to * across the entire width of the weft.

Step 1: down

Step 2: up and pick-up stick

Step 3: down

Step 4: up and pick-up stick

Step 5: down

Step 6: up and pick-up stick

Step 7: down

Step 8: up

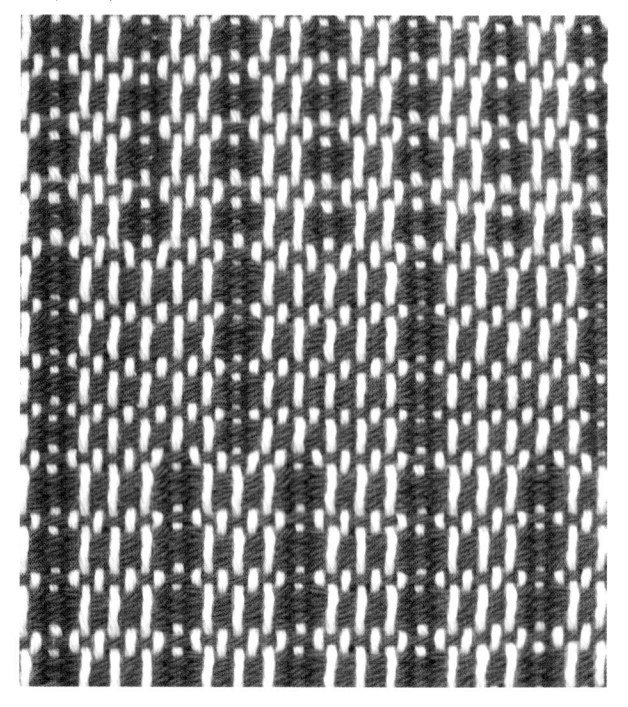

Combinations of Warp and Weft Floats

Pattern 1 – "Honeycomb" Effect: *1 up, 1 down*, repeat from * to * across the entire width of the weft.

Step 1: down
Step 2: up and pick-up stick
Step 3: down
Step 4: up
Step 5: pick-up stick
Step 6: up

Pick-up stick pattern 2: *3 up, 1 down*, repeat from * to * across the entire width of the weft.

Step 1: up
Step 2: pick-up stick
Step 3: up
Step 4: pick-up stick
Step 5: up
Step 6: down
Step 7: up and pick-up stick
Step 8: down
Step 9: up and pick-up stick
Step 10: down

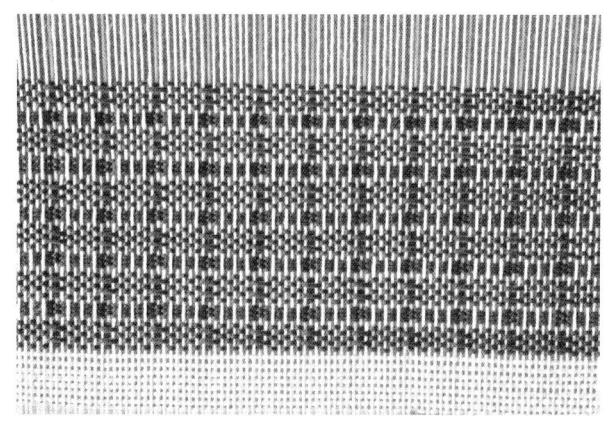

Other Types of Structures - 81

Designs with Inlays

Using your pick-up stick more freely, you can create inlays, decorative elements that are independent of the rest of the weave and that can be placed at will.

With the pick-up stick, it is quick and easy to create patterns across the entire width of the fabric. This, however, is not all good news, as it is impossible, for example, with a single pick-up stick, to weave columns of two different colors in the same row. Nevertheless, you can manually insert sections of different colors to achieve the desired result. While this method is more time-consuming than the pick-up stick, the creative freedom it offers is well worth the effort.

Inlays are made, not with shuttles, but with small, pre-made balls. You will need one ball for each block you make.

Pick-up stick pattern: *1 down, 1 up*, repeat from * to * across the entire width of the weft.

Inlay blocks: blocks of 3 floats, 3 spaced floats, in two colors.

1 Work a few rows of plain weave with your basic main shuttle.

2 **Place the heddle in the neutral position**; place the pick-up stick just behind the heddle, alternating 1 thread above and 1 thread below the stick, and turn it on its edge. This will open up a new shed in front of the heddle.

3 Work from right to left. Insert the end of your first ball of yarn under 3 threads in the new shed, where you want to make your first block/ inlay. Let the rest of the ball hang on the front of the weave.

4 Leave a space of 3 free threads and insert the end of your second ball under the next 3 threads of the new shed. Also let the rest of the second ball hang on the front of the weave.

5 Continue in this way until you have inserted the end of each ball of yarn at the location of the planned blocks. All the balls are on the front of the weave. So, if you planned for 5 blocks, you now have 5 balls on the front of the weave, in addition to your shuttle for the base fabric.

6 Turn the pick-up stick flat and push it toward the back of the loom to close the extra shed.

7 **Place the heddle in the up position** and work at least one row of plain weave. You can go back and forth as many times as you like.

8 **Place the heddle in the neutral position**, and again move the pick-up stick so it is just behind the heddle and turn it on its edge. This time, work from left to right. For each block, again insert the yarn from the balls used previously under the 3 same threads as in steps 4 and 5. Continue to let the balls hang on the front of the weave.

9 Continue in this way until you reach the desired height of your blocks. Then cut the thread from the ball and pass the tail to the back of the fabric.

10 When you've finished weaving, use a needle to weave in the thread tails at the beginning and end of each block into the back side of the fabric.

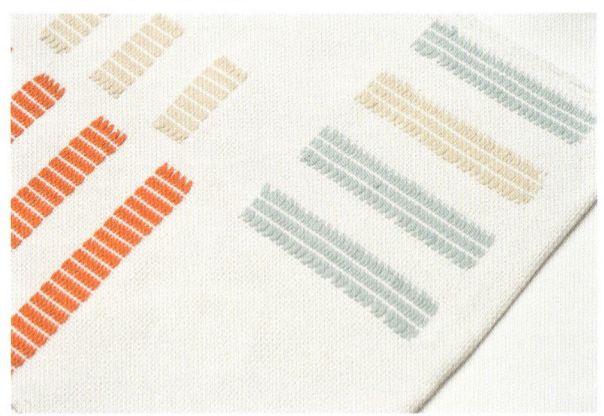

Patterns with Supplemental Warp

Quite simple to make, the supplemental warp technique adds a lot of interest and possibilities to the range of weaves you can make.

For this method, warp the loom with two separate warps:

- a **base warp**, as for a conventional warp,
- **supplemental yarn** to be placed above the base warp at certain points. This will be used to create a pattern during weaving. You can place this freely according to your own design ideas: there are no rules about spacing or placement of this warp.

Please Note

This supplemental yarn will only be warped through the slots, not the eyes!

Warping the Loom

We rely on the direct warping technique detailed on page 24.

1 Prepare the materials for direct warping and load your basic warp onto the loom as described on pages 24 to 27, up to step 8.

2 Add the supplemental warp threads above some of those already in place, according to the desired pattern, passing them through the heddle slots only. Those slots will then contain 4 warp ends instead of 2. To do this, tie the extra yarn around the tie rod, facing the slots in which they will be placed. Cut and knot them at the end of this space, and tie them again at the next point, so as not to have too many threads crossing each other.

Placement of Supplemental Warp

There is no rule about where to place the supplemental warp threads, but they're usually placed a bit spaced out from each other.

3 Wind your two warps together, as you would for conventional weaving (see page 29).

4 Now thread the eyes. During this step, ignore the supplemental warp threads; they'll simply stay doubled in the slots. Thus, some slots will have 3 threads: the base warp + 2 supplemental warp threads.

5 Complete warping by following the instructions on pages 31 and 32.

6 Once warping is complete, insert your pick-up stick behind the heddle, under all the supplemental warp threads but above the others. Then push it toward the back of the loom.

Weaving with Supplemental Warp Threads

Now that your warp threads are in place, separated by the pick-up stick behind the rigid heddle, all that's left to do is weave. The position of the pick-up stick will determine whether the supplemental warp threads will be in the base fabric or not. They will be if the pick-up stick remains toward the back of the loom, but if the pick-up stick is just behind the heddle, not turned, the supplemental warp threads will remain above the base fabric.

The resulting floats can be any length you like. You can even cut them off at the end of the weave to create a small fringe on your fabric; the choice is yours! Note, however, that floats that are too long are always more likely to snag.

You can also insert objects into these floats, as I did for the large woven trivet on page 136, shown below.

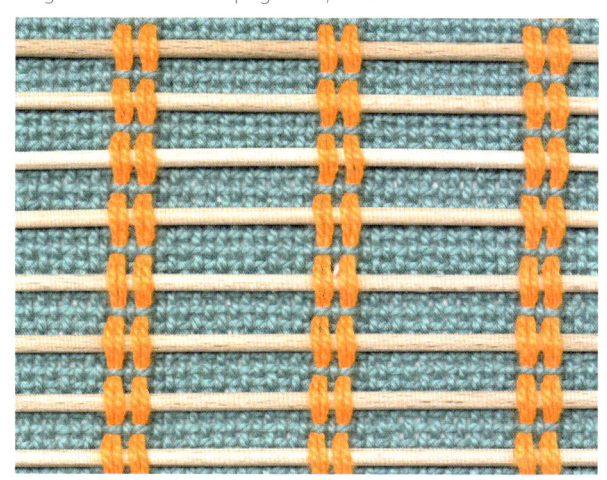

Other Types of Structures - 83

Overshot-Style Patterns

The last technique using a single pick-up stick was recently described in Myra Wood's book, *Crazyshot! Creative Overshot Weaving on a Rigid Heddle Loom*. It resembles overshot weaving, a classic technique performed on shaft looms. The idea is to create patterns with a thick thread on top of a thinner base fabric by inserting the pick-up stick in front of the heddle on every row.

Inserting the pick-up stick on every row is what makes it possible to create freeform patterns, diagonals, or diamonds, etc. Such complex patterns would normally be impossible with a rigid heddle loom. The only drawback is the need to insert the pick-up stick for each row, as this is extremely time-consuming and requires a great deal of concentration.

Here are some basic principles of this type of weaving.

- Warp the loom with a thin yarn and weave, always alternating:
  - one row of plain weave with the same thin yarn as the base fabric
  - a pattern row with a yarn 2 or 3 times thicker.
- For the pattern row, always insert the pick-up stick in front of the rigid heddle (placed in the neutral position) following a diagram.
- When weaving the plain weave between pattern rows, make sure you always alternate between the up and down positions of the heddle. Use my tip on page 46 to always know where you are. The diagram pattern alone requires a great deal of concentration, and without a simple way of getting your bearings in the plain weave, you're likely to get lost very quickly.

How to Read the Diagram

- The diagram shows only the pattern rows; the plain weave rows between each of them are not shown but must still be woven.
- It is read from right to left and from bottom to top.
- Each column corresponds to a warp thread, each row to a row of weaving. Each square indicates the position of the pick-up stick:
  - white square: place pick-up stick under the warp thread.
  - colored square: place pick-up stick over the warp thread.

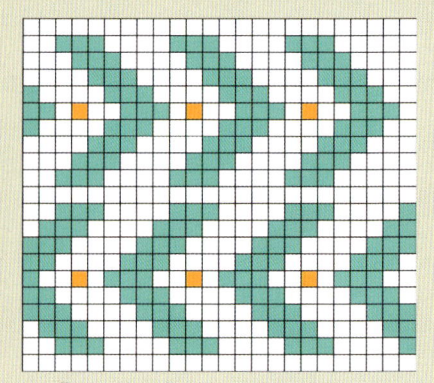

Example of an overshot diagram

Weaving with Two Pick-Up Sticks

To go even further in creating your patterns, you can also work with two pick-up sticks at the same time.

The problem with this technique is that you can leave only one of the two pick-up sticks in place during the entire weaving. The second pick-up stick must be removed and reinserted as needed, which of course takes a little longer.

Inserting Pick-Up Sticks

1 Insert pick-up stick A just behind the heddle, with the heddle in the down position, as in conventional weaving.

2 Insert pick-up stick B just behind the first, following the second pattern.

3 Once you've woven the pattern for pick-up stick A, remove it from the warp to weave pattern B.

4 After weaving pattern B, reinsert pick-up stick A in front of the other. A typical pattern with two pick-up sticks is the honeycomb pattern found below.

Honeycomb Pattern

This pattern creates "rounded cells." To emphasize the pattern, use a colored or thicker yarn for step 1, which creates the border of the cells.

Pick-up stick A pattern: *5 up, 5 down*, repeat from * to * across the entire width of the weft.

Pick-up stick B pattern: *5 down, 5 up*, repeat from * to * across the entire width of the weft.

Step 1: down (border yarn)
Step 2: up and pick-up stick A
Step 3: down
Step 4: up and pick-up stick A
Step 5: down
Step 6: up and pick-up stick A
Step 7: down
Step 8: up and pick-up stick A
Step 9: down (border yarn)
Step 10: up and pick-up stick B
Step 11: down
Step 12: up and pick-up stick B
Step 13: down
Step 14: up and pick-up stick B
Step 15: down
Step 16: up and pick-up stick B

Replacing One of the Pick-Up Sticks with a Heddle Rod

As we explained earlier, the problem with weaving with two pick-up sticks is that you must remove one to weave the second pattern, then reinsert it later. It is tedious and time-consuming.

A fairly simple way to avoid this is to replace one of the pick-up sticks with a heddle rod, suspended with bits of string. The advantage of this method is that the cotton loops (the heddles), which attach the wooden rod to the warp threads used in the second pattern, don't interfere with the movement of the pick-up stick in place. You can therefore push the pick-up stick behind the heddle and turn it, as you would with a conventional weave, when you weave the second pattern, lifting the wooden rod and, with it, the warp threads attached to it. This allows you to leave the rod in place throughout the weaving process and save an enormous amount of time.

For this technique, you will need:

- a wooden rod, longer than the width of your weft,
- cotton string, strong but thin, to create the heddles,
- scotch or masking tape.

1 Cut as many pieces of string as you have warp threads to lift for the second pattern. Try to cut all the strands to the same length: around 10 to 12 inches.

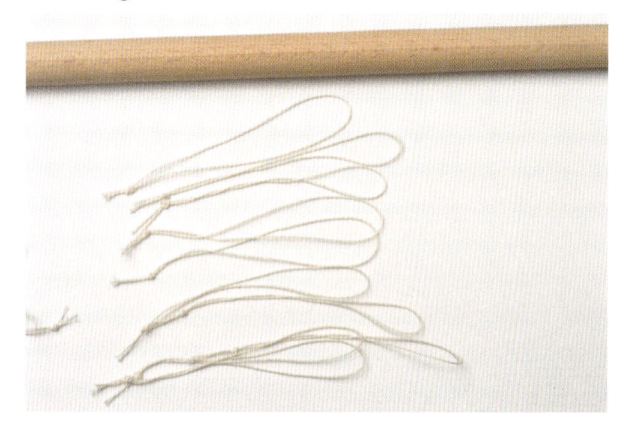

2 Tie the two ends of each piece of string together so that each knot forms a loop. In the same way, try to keep the loops identical in size.

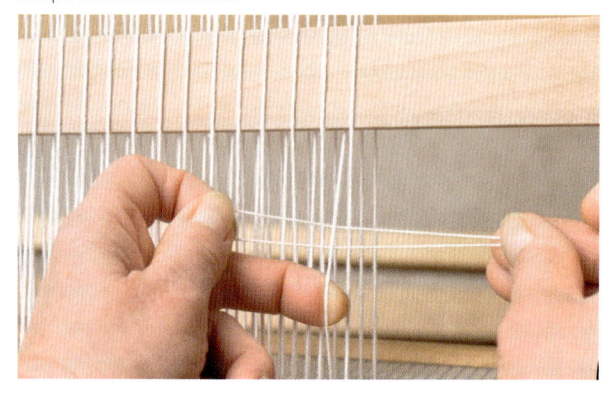

3 Place a loop under the first thread to be lifted to make your second pattern.

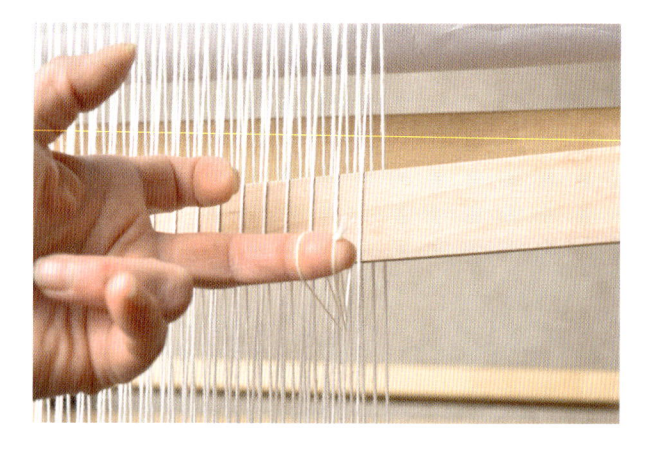

4 Fold it in half and point the ends upward so that you have a loop on each side of the warp thread to be lifted.

5 Insert the wooden rod through the two loops thus formed.

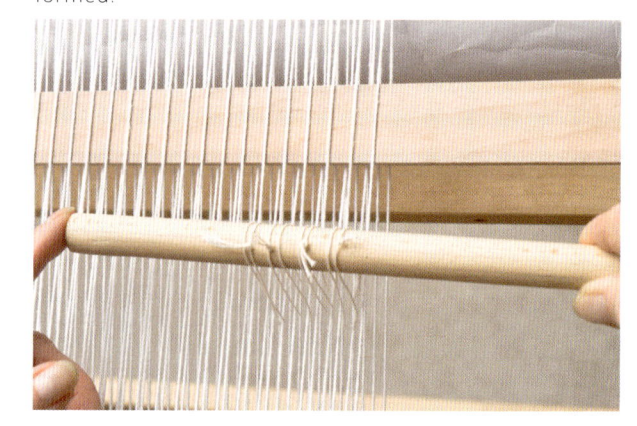

86 - Complete Guide to Rigid Heddle Weaving

6 Continue in this manner along the entire width of the warp, inserting a string heddle around each warp end to be lifted to create the second pattern, inserting the rod through them as you go.

7 When all the heddles are on the rod, secure them with a piece of tape to prevent them from slipping during weaving. Using this rod, you can now raise or lower the threads of your second pattern. When it's time to weave your second pattern, simply lift the rod with one hand and, with it, the warp threads. To work the opposite pattern, leave the rod "on hold" behind the heddle.

Weaving with Two Heddles

Another way to expand your range of weaves on a rigid heddle loom is to use two heddles at the same time.

A single heddle on a rigid heddle loom acts like two shafts on a hand loom. The extra heddle is equivalent to an additional shaft, enabling you to weave **three-shaft designs**, rather than the four-shaft designs as you might think. To do that, you must also add one or even two pick-up sticks.

In fact, it is possible to weave with three or four heddles at the same time, but I'm only going to mention two-heddle techniques.

Nowadays, the heddle support block is often already designed to accommodate two heddles at a time. If this is not the case, you can buy a replacement block.

The second heddle has different functions:

- It can be used to make finer fabrics, as the density can be doubled.
- It makes it possible to weave twill and other patterns that normally require three or four shafts. However, this requires the use of additional pick-up sticks.
- It can be used for double weaving, to double the width, for example. This also requires additional pick-up sticks.

Finer Fabrics

The heddles must be warped in distinct ways to match the technique to be used, and above all they must be the same density.

The simplest method, described below, allows you to produce a finer fabric, as the use of two heddles makes it possible to double the density. Two 12.5-dent (50/10) heddles, for example, produce a 25 epi (10 ends/cm) fabric, while two 10-dent (40/10) heddles produce a 20 epi (8 ends/cm) fabric.

In this configuration, you can produce most woven patterns with a pick-up stick. The second heddle acts as the pick-up stick.

We rely on the direct warping technique described on page 24.

1 Prepare the material for direct warping. For the moment, only put the rear heddle in place; this is the one you will warp first.

2 Thread the rear heddle following steps 1 to 9 on pages 24 to 28. The only difference is in step 7. For this step, **pull 2 loops through each slot**, instead of one, so that each slot contains 4 threads instead of 2.

3 Wind the warp and cut the loops as described on pages 28 to 29 (steps 10 to 13).

4 Pull the rightmost thread in the slot through the eye to the right and do the same for the rest of the heddle, so that only 3 threads remain in a slot.

5 Now place the second heddle in front of the other, in the heddle block. Make sure that the slots of both heddles are aligned.

6 Thread the warp through the front heddle.

- Pull the thread you've just placed in the eye of the rear heddle through the slot on the right-hand side of the front heddle.
- There are 3 warp ends left in each rear slot. Separate them as follows.
   - Pull the rightmost thread through the slot on the right of the front heddle. This is the same slot where you already have the thread from the eye.
   - Pull the middle thread through the eye on the right of the front heddle.
   - Pull the thread on the left through the slot to the left on the front heddle.

7 At the end, you must have in both heddles:
- 1 thread in each eye,
- 3 threads in each slot.

8 Make sure that no threads cross between the two heddles. To do this, test all possible positions of the heddles and see if the shed opens correctly.

9 Now you can finish warping by attaching the threads to the front bar.

Warping fine fabric with two heddles

Weaving with two heddles for a fine plain weave fabric is quite easy: simply raise and lower both heddles at the same time.

Twill

For a twill weave, warp your two heddles as you would for a finer fabric (see page 87), and make sure you have two pick-up sticks.

Pick-up stick A pattern: With both heddles in the down position, place the second warp thread on the pick-up stick, then every other one.

Pick-up stick B pattern: With both heddles in the down position, place all warp ends not on the first pick-up stick on the second one.

Step 1: front heddle up

Step 2: both heddles in neutral position + pick-up stick A.

Step 3: rear heddle up

Step 4: both heddles in neutral position + pick-up stick B.

Theo Moorman Technique

Theo Moorman, an English artist, devised a rather surprising technique, which I love, for incorporating freeform patterns above the base fabric.

The principle is much the same as the one for supplemental warp (see page 83). Very thin thread, such as sewing thread, is warped at the same time as the normal warp. These "invisible" threads are not part of the fabric's structure, so they can move freely. So, when you lift them up, you can inlay a weft pattern yarn across any portion of the warp to "draw" whatever you envision.

> **Notes**
> - This technique requires an additional pick-up stick.
> - The front heddle creates the basic plain weave fabric. The base warp threads are distributed as usual between the slots and eyes.
> - The rear heddle is used to move the supplemental warp threads used to create the pattern. The density of the heddle is halved, so when warping the loom, place the thread in only every other slot.

We use the direct warping technique described on page 24.

1 Prepare the materials for direct warping. Place both heddles in the block; you'll be warping them at the same time.

2 Thread both heddles, alternating as follows:
- one loop of base warp in one slot,
- one loop of the base warp + one loop of the supplemental warp in the next slot.

To do this, start on the right with a loop of base warp only, and work your way to the left, adding the supplemental warp starting in the next slot. Every other slot now contains 4 threads instead of 2. Wind the warp as usual and cut the loops open.

3 Thread the eyes of the front heddle as usual, using the base warp thread. Pull the right-hand thread through the right-hand eye while the left-hand thread remains in the slot.

4 Take the right-hand thread of the supplemental warp from the rear heddle and remove it from the slot. Insert it first into the eye to the right in the rear heddle, then into the right slot of the front heddle.

5 Check that there are no crossed threads between the two heddles.

6 At the end of warping you should have:
- in the back heddle: every other eye/slot contains the supplemental warp thread,
- in the front heddle: only every other eye/slot contains warp threads, but each eye/slot is warped with the base warp thread and the supplemental one.

7 You can then finish warping by attaching the threads to the front bar.

Theo Moorman warping

To weave using this Theo Moorman technique, you need to insert the pick-up stick. Place both heddles in the down position and take **all the supplemental warp threads from the slots on the pick-up stick**. Then weave as follows, inserting your pattern yarn every other row wherever you like (or your pattern yarns, as of course you can also create several patterns at the same time).

Other Types of Structures - 89

Step 1: two heddles down (base yarn)

Step 2: rear heddle up (pattern thread)

Step 3: two heddles up (base yarn)

Step 4: two heddles in neutral position + pick-up stick (pattern thread)

Double Weave

It is possible to weave two layers of fabric, one on top of the other, which is called "double weave."

These two layers can be connected on both sides to create a **tube**, or they can be joined on one side only, forming a double width fabric. Both layers can also be totally separate during weaving or mingle at some points during weaving, with the layer at the bottom becoming visible at the top, while the top layer appears at the bottom.

For this type of weaving on the rigid heddle loom, you need two heddles with the same density and two pick-up sticks. If you want to be able to switch the top and bottom fabrics, you'll need four pick-up sticks.

Pay Attention to Density

As you are weaving two separate layers at the same time, you need to calculate the density as you would for a single heddle weave, and not by dividing it by two as we saw on page 21. In other words, if you have two 10-dent (40/10) heddles, take a yarn that matches the density of 10 and not the density of 20.

Often, in double weaving, the two layers are two different colors. The warping below calls for a dark yarn for the first heddle (front) and a light color for the second (back).

We use the direct warping technique described on page 24.

1 Prepare the materials needed for direct warping. For the moment, only set the back heddle in the block as this is the one you will thread first.

2 Thread the back heddle following steps 1 to 9 on pages 24 to 28. The only difference is in step 7, where **you must pull 2 loops through each slot** instead of one, so that each slot contains 4 warp ends instead of 2.

3 Wind the warp and cut the loops as described on pages 28 and 29 (steps 10 to 13).

4 Pull the rightmost light thread in the slot, through the eye on the right, and do the same for the rest of the heddle, so that only 3 threads remain in the slot.

5 Now place the other heddle in front, in the block provided. Make sure that the slots of both heddles are aligned.

6 Thread the front heddle.

- Pull the thread you've just placed in the eye of the back heddle through the slot on the right in the front heddle.
- Pull the second light thread through the same slot.
- Pull the first dark thread through the next eye, to the left of the slot with the two light threads.
- Pull the second dark thread through the next slot to the left of the eye just threaded.

7 At the end, you should have in both heddles:

- one light thread in each eye of the back heddle,
- one dark thread in each eye of the front heddle,
- three threads in each rear slot,
- two light threads and one dark thread alternating in the front heddle slots.

90 - Complete Guide to Rigid Heddle Weaving

Check that your yarn does not cross between the two heddles. Test all possible heddle positions to make sure each shed opens correctly.

8 Finish warping by attaching the threads to the front bar.

Warping for double weave

Weaving Two Separate Layers

Pick-up stick A pattern: With both heddles in the down position, pick up every second thread on the pick-up stick starting with the second dark thread. This pick-up stick will remain throughout weaving.

Pick-up stick B pattern: With both heddles in the up position, pull pick-up stick A toward the heddle and slide pick-up stick B into the small shed created at the bottom between the light-colored yarns. This separates the light yarns for weaving the lower layer. This pick-up stick will be re-placed during each sequence.

Weaving Two Separate Layers with Dark Dominant Top

You need two shuttles, one with a light weft and the second with a dark weft.

Light lower layer

Step 1: pick-up stick B, light weft

Step 2: heddle 1 (front) down, light weft

Dark upper layer

Step 3: heddle 2 (back) up, dark weft

Step 4: pick-up stick A, dark weft

Weaving Two Separate Layers with Light Dominant Top

You need two additional pick-up sticks (C and D); pick-up sticks A and B can be left in place for later.

Pick-up stick C Pattern: With both heddles in the down position, place every second light yarn on the pick-up stick, starting with the first one.

Pick-up stick D Pattern: With both heddles in the up position, pull pick-up stick C toward the heddle and slide pick-up stick D into the small shed created at the bottom between the dark threads. This separates the dark threads for weaving the lower layer.

Dark lower layer

Step 1: pick-up stick D, dark weft

Step 2: heddle 2 (back) down, dark weft

Dark upper layer

Step 3: heddle 1 (front) up, light weft

Step 4: pick-up stick C, light weft

Weaving Two Connected Layers

Double-Width Weave, Joined on One Side

You only need one shuttle. The join is made on the side opposite to the one where you start.

For a double width, weave: lower layer, upper layer, upper layer, lower layer.

Step 1: pick-up stick B

Step 2: heddle 2 (back) up

Step 3: pick-up stick A

Step 4: heddle 1 (front) down

Tube Weave Joined on Both Sides

You only need one shuttle.

For one tube, weave: lower layer, upper layer, lower layer, upper layer.

Step 1: pick-up stick B

Step 2: heddle 2 (back) up

Step 3: heddle 1 (front) down

Step 4: pick-up stick A

Other Types of Structures - 91

Focus on the Norwegian Krokbragd Technique

Last but not least, this technique is my favorite, the one for which I really got into weaving: krokbragd!

I know it's a weird name and nobody knows how to pronounce it properly. Nevertheless, it is my favorite weaving technique because its patterns are so beautiful.

Krokbragd is a traditional Norwegian technique in which the **weft is predominant**. It produces thick, dense fabrics, mainly used for rugs, cushions, and bedspreads. You need to beat with the heddle until you can't see your warp at all, which makes weaving quite time-consuming. This is not a technique recommended for impatient people.

Krokbragd is in itself quite simple to execute. You always repeat the same three steps, no variation there. The only thing that changes during the weaving process is the color you use.

You can weave krokbragd with either **two heddles** or **two pick-up sticks**. If you choose two pick-up sticks, you can make things even easier by **replacing one of the pick-up sticks with a heddle rod**, as explained on page 85. The rod can remain in place throughout the weaving process, unlike the second pick-up stick, which must be replaced every three rows. The rod saves an enormous amount of time. Personally, I'd much rather use a pick-up stick and a rod than two heddles, but do your own tests to find out which way suits you best.

The two main difficulties with krokbragd are finding the right density and making pretty edges.

• **Density:** As the weft is dominant, you'll need to cover the warp completely and, to make this possible, space the warp threads further apart. Be careful, however, since if the warp threads are too far apart and the beating too light, the fabric will be unstable.

Unfortunately, there is no calculation to determine the density of this type of fabric. You can base your calculation on that of plain weave (see page 20) and use a heddle that is one or two sizes smaller, but sampling is essential.

With a rigid heddle loom, you may not be able to beat enough for this technique. Use a hair comb to help you out every 5 or 6 rows.

- **Selvedges:** The first difficulty with the selvedges is that with this technique, they tend to shrink. So use a temple, especially if you want to make a rug, for example. And be sure to weave using the 45-degree angle (see page 39).

The second difficulty is color management. I always try to show on the edge the color I am using in two of the three steps. As for the second color thread, I bring it out and insert it before the edge, so that it remains invisible. This becomes difficult when using three colors at the same time.

Other Recommendations

Remember to beat firmly so that the warp is no longer visible.

Krokbragd with Two Heddles

Warping

We use the direct warping technique described on page 24.

1 Prepare the materials for direct warping. For the moment, only place the rear heddle, as this is the one you will warp first.

2 Thread the back heddle by following steps 1 to 9 on pages 24 to 28. At the end, you have one thread in each slot and each eye. For perfect symmetry, remove the first thread on the right from the eye and leave it behind the loom, without using it.

3 Wind the warp and cut the loops as described on pages 28 and 29 (steps 10 to 13).

4 Now place the second heddle in front of the other, in the heddle block. Make sure that the slots of both heddles are aligned.

5 Take the first thread from the first slot (the thread from the first eye is not used) and place it in the eye to the right in the front heddle.

- Place the second thread of the rear heddle in the next slot, to the left of the first, and leave the next eye empty. Place the next two threads in the following slot.
- Repeat *1 in eye, 1 in slot, 2 in slot, 1 eye empty* across the entire width and finish with 1 thread in the eye.

6 You can then finish warping by knotting the threads on the front rod.

Warping krokbragd

Focus on the Norwegian Krokbragd Technique - 93

Weaving

> **Steps to Repeat to Create a Pattern Row**
> 1. Heddles A and B up.
> 2. Heddle A (front) down.
> 3. Heddle B (back) down.

The only thing that changes is the color you use for each step. You can use:
- a single color for all steps,
- one color for two of the steps and a second for the remaining step,
- one color for each step, in a specific order,
- a different color for each step, the order of which changes with each repetition.

Each time, you create a new pattern.

Krokbragd with a Heddle, a Pick-Up Stick, and a Heddle Rod

Warping

Warping for this version is identical to that described on page 24.

After attaching the threads to the front rod, insert the pick-up stick and the heddle rod. To do this, proceed as follows.

1 Place the heddle in the down position.

2 Behind the heddle, insert a pick-up stick with the pattern "1 thread above/1 thread below."

3 Then insert the heddle rod (as explained on page 85), taking the threads not yet on the pick-up stick (i.e., every second thread) onto the rod.

If you prefer to use a second pick-up stick rather than the rod, this is perfectly possible, but you will need to remove and reinsert the first pick-up stick A each time you weave with B, as explained on page 85.

Example of a krokbragd with a flames pattern.

As explained opposite, always repeat the same three steps to form a pattern row. It is the colors used for each row that will define the pattern. Note that the **color you use for step 3 will appear twice as often in the pattern as the previous ones**, as this is when half the threads are raised and lowered.

Weaving

> **Steps to Repeat to Create a Pattern Row**
> 1. Heddle up + pick-up stick A in front.
> 2. Heddle up + lift heddle rod (or lift pick-up stick B in front if you opt for a second pick-up stick).
> 3. Heddle down.

The only thing that changes is the color you use in each step. You can use:
- a single color for all steps,
- one color for two of the steps and a second color for the remaining step,
- one color per step, in the same order,
- a different color for each step, the order of which changes with each repetition.

Each time, you create a new pattern.

Reading a Krokbragd Pattern

Krokbragd patterns are generally described as follows: the color used for each step in the pattern row is indicated, as well as the number of times the color choice must be repeated. G = green; W = white; R = red.

To perform the first operation "Weave GWW pattern row 5 times," use green for step 1 and white for steps 2 and 3 to obtain the first pattern row of the weave. Repeat this row 4 more times before continuing.

1. Weave GWW pattern row 5 times.
2. Weave GWG pattern row 5 times.
3. Weave RGG pattern row 5 times.
4. Weave RGR pattern row 5 times.
5. Weave RGR pattern row 5 times.
6. Weave WRR pattern row 5 times.
7. Weave WRW pattern row 5 times.

Here are other examples of patterns.

Focus on the Norwegian Krokbragd Technique - 95

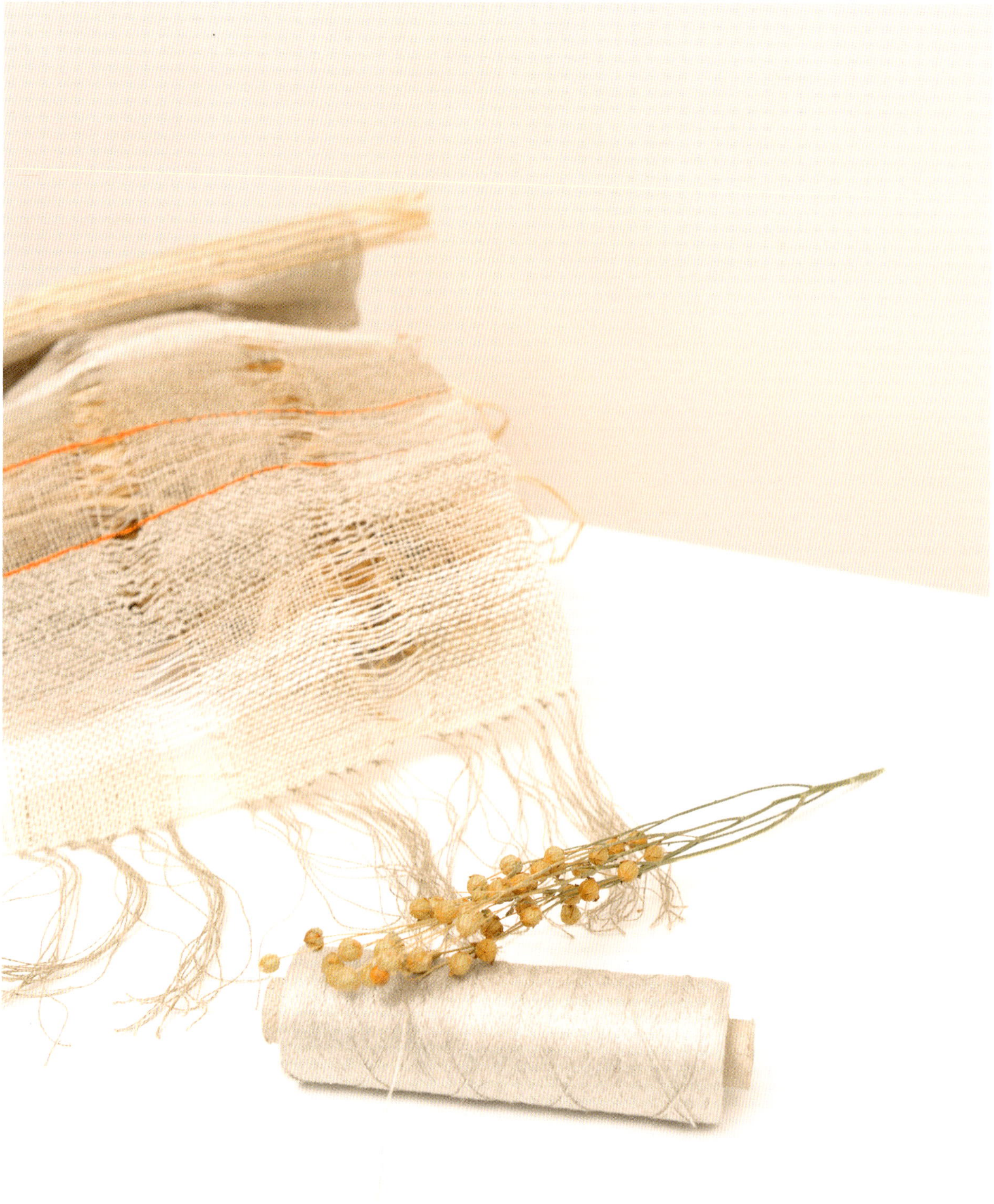

11 PROJECTS TO MOVE FORWARD IN YOUR WEAVING ADVENTURE

Now it is time to put your knowledge into practice and make some beautiful projects.

A fringed scarf, origami bag, colorful pouch, assorted dish towels, beautiful textured pillow, bright set of placemats, natural wood trivet, or a set of geometric coasters—here you will find elegant and timeless designs to suit all tastes.

Fringed Scarf

This simple project will give you confidence in how to use a rigid heddle loom. This scarf is very easy to weave, but the use of hand-dyed and variegated yarns makes it unique, and the effects are always surprising and captivating. Watch out, you'll be hooked!

Technique: Plain weave (page 34)
Sett: 10 ends per inch (4 threads/cm)
Warping dimensions: 16 in. × 2½ yd. (40 × 220 cm)
Final dimensions: 15 in. × 75 in. (38 × 190 cm), including fringe

Difficulty: Beginner
Time required: 8 hours
Sewing: No

Tools and Materials
- Loom + warping materials (page 24)
- Shuttle
- Needle
- A few yards of thick cotton yarn
- Fringe twister (optional)

Yarn
Hedgehog Fibres Sock Yarn
- Warp: 1 skein in Clay
- Weft: 1 skein in Liebling

Notes
- Although the ideal density is really 12.5 epi (5 threads/cm), I opted for a 10-dent (40/10) reed to create a more flowing scarf with a nice drape.
- You can use solid-color, plainer wools, but the result will be less spectacular. Try semisolid or speckled wools to create unique effects.

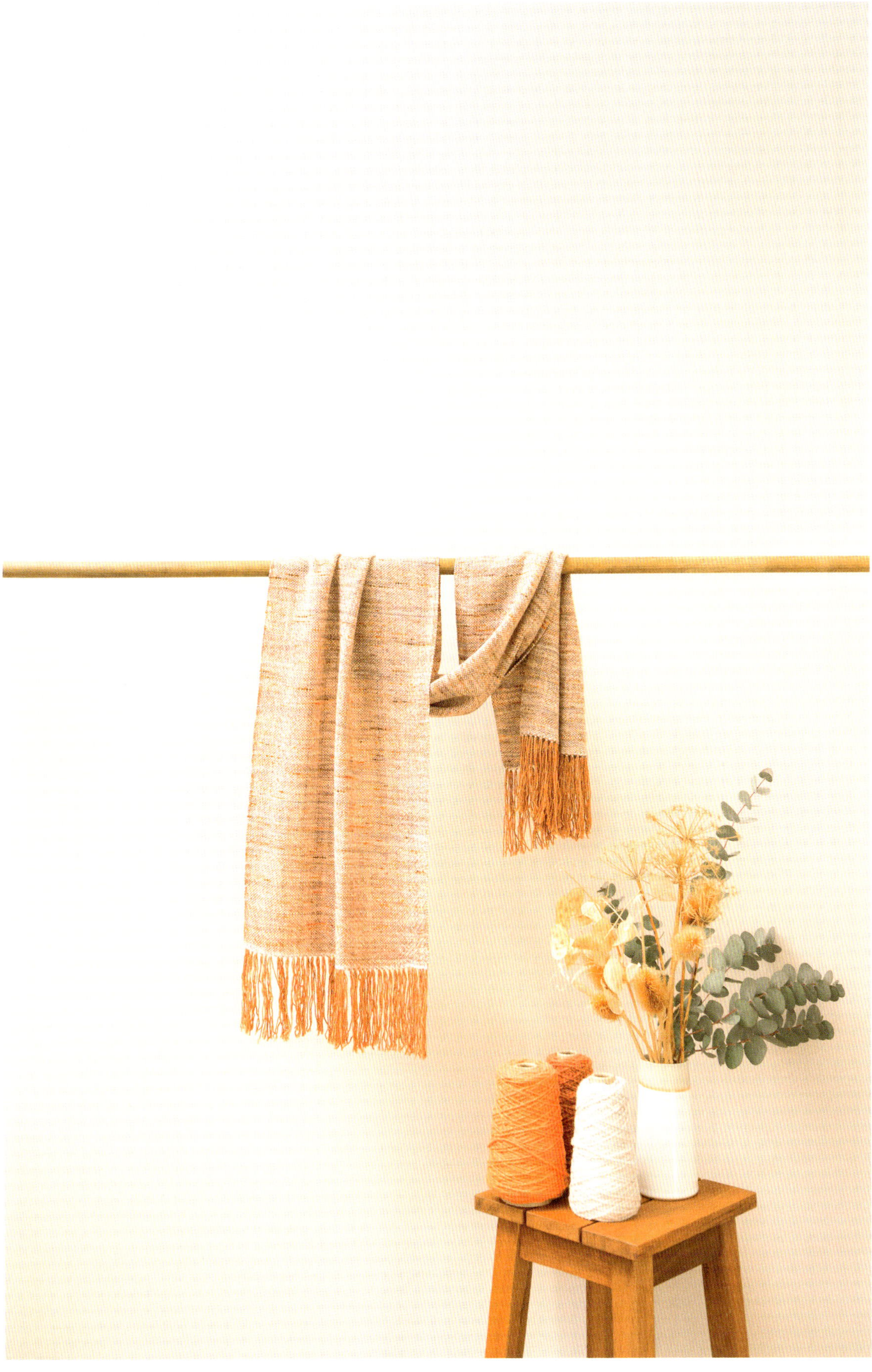

Instructions

1 Wind on a warp 16 inches wide by 2½ yards long (40 × 220 cm) with the color Clay using the 10-dent (40/10) heddle. Carefully center your warp on the loom.

2 After evening out the warp with thick cotton yarn, prepare a shuttle with the Liebling colorway.

3 Work the first 4 rows in plain weave with the Liebling colorway, leaving a tail of at least 30 in. (80 cm) when starting the weave.

4 Thread this tail through the needle and hemstitch the end (see page 43).

5 Continue weaving the plain weave until there is at least 30 in. (80 cm) left on your skein. Be careful with your selvedges and always beat the weft in from a 45-degree angle.

6 Weave a final row from left to right.

7 Thread the yarn end in the needle and hemstitch the other end.

8 Cut your scarf from the loom at the top, leaving at least 6 in. (15 cm) of fringe. The hemstitch secures the weave, so there is no need to tie knots.

9 Unwind your scarf from the front beam. Untie the knots at the beginning and remove the thick cotton yarn used to even out the warp.

10 You can leave the fringe as is or twist several strands together. In either case, even out the length with a ruler.

11 Wash the scarf, lay it flat to dry, and iron if necessary.

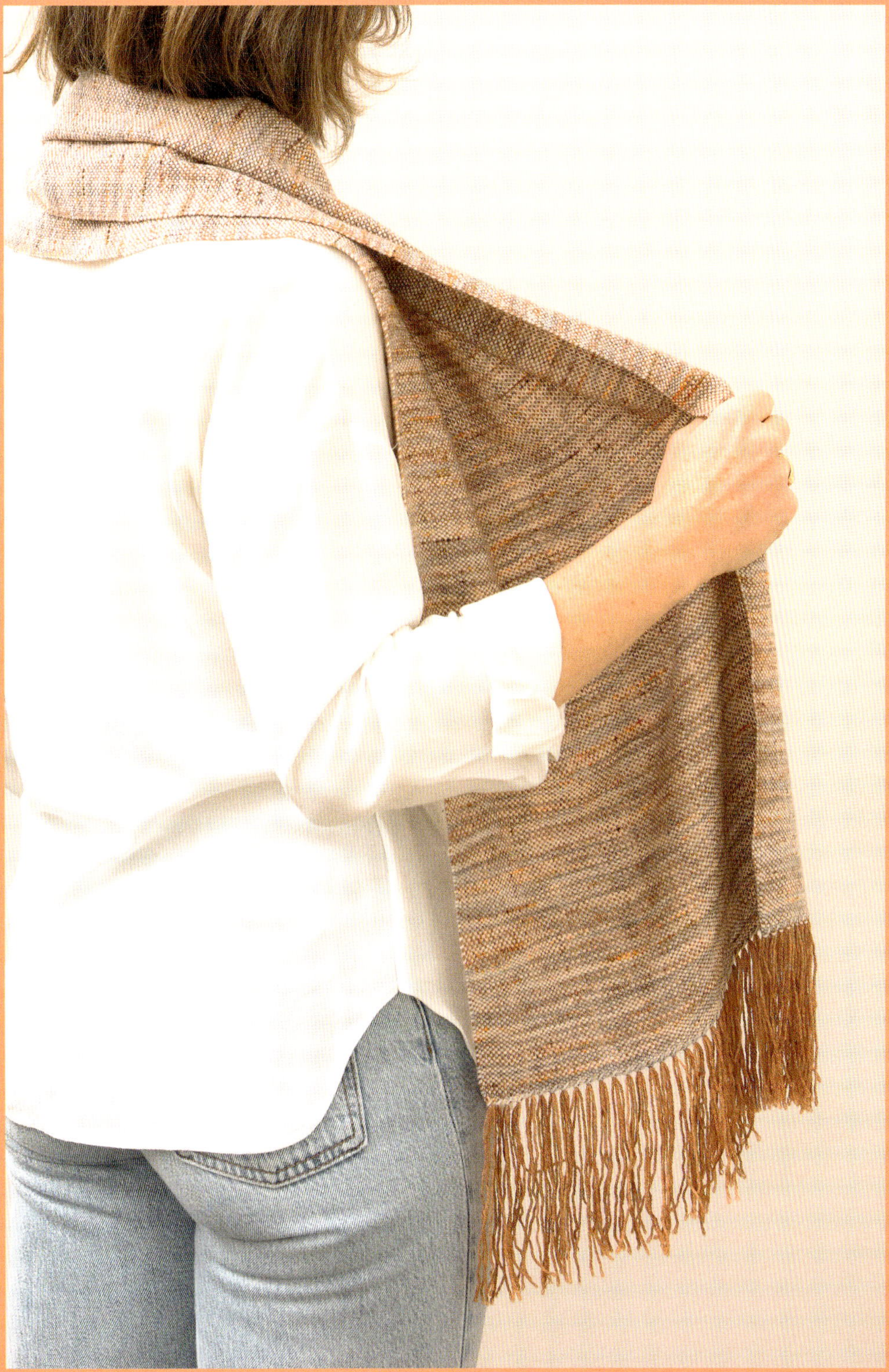

Origami Bag

The origami bag is one of my favorites. All you do is weave a large rectangle—the clever folds create this smart design! Play with the diagonals by putting a pattern on just one part, as I did here with the stripes.

Techniques: Plain weave (page 34), stripes (page 53), and texture (page 53)
Sett: 12.5 ends per inch (5 threads/cm)
Warping dimensions: 14 in. × 1½ yd. (35 × 140 cm)
Final dimensions: 19 in. × 24 in. (48 × 60 cm), including strap

Difficulty: Beginner
Time required: 8 hours
Sewing: Yes, preferably with sewing machine

Tools and Materials
- Loom + warping materials (page 24)
- 4 shuttles
- Needle
- Fabric for the lining and strap: 16 in. × 48 in. (40 × 120 cm)
- Sewing machine

Yarn
- Warp: CaMaRose Yaku, 2 skeins Rahvid
- Weft:
  - Dominant color: CaMaRose Økologisk Hverdagsuld, 2 skeins Rahvid
  - Stripes:
    - Hedgehog Fibres Sock Yarn, 87.5 yd. (80 m) Fool's Gold
    - Funem Natural Silk Yarn, 87.5 yd. (80 m)
    - Alysse Creations Silk Bouclé, 87.5 yd. (80 m)

Notes
- For folding to work, **the length must be 3 times the width**.
- If you want to include a different effect or material to highlight the diagonal construction, do this either on the first third of the weave (14 in./35 cm) or on the remaining two-thirds.

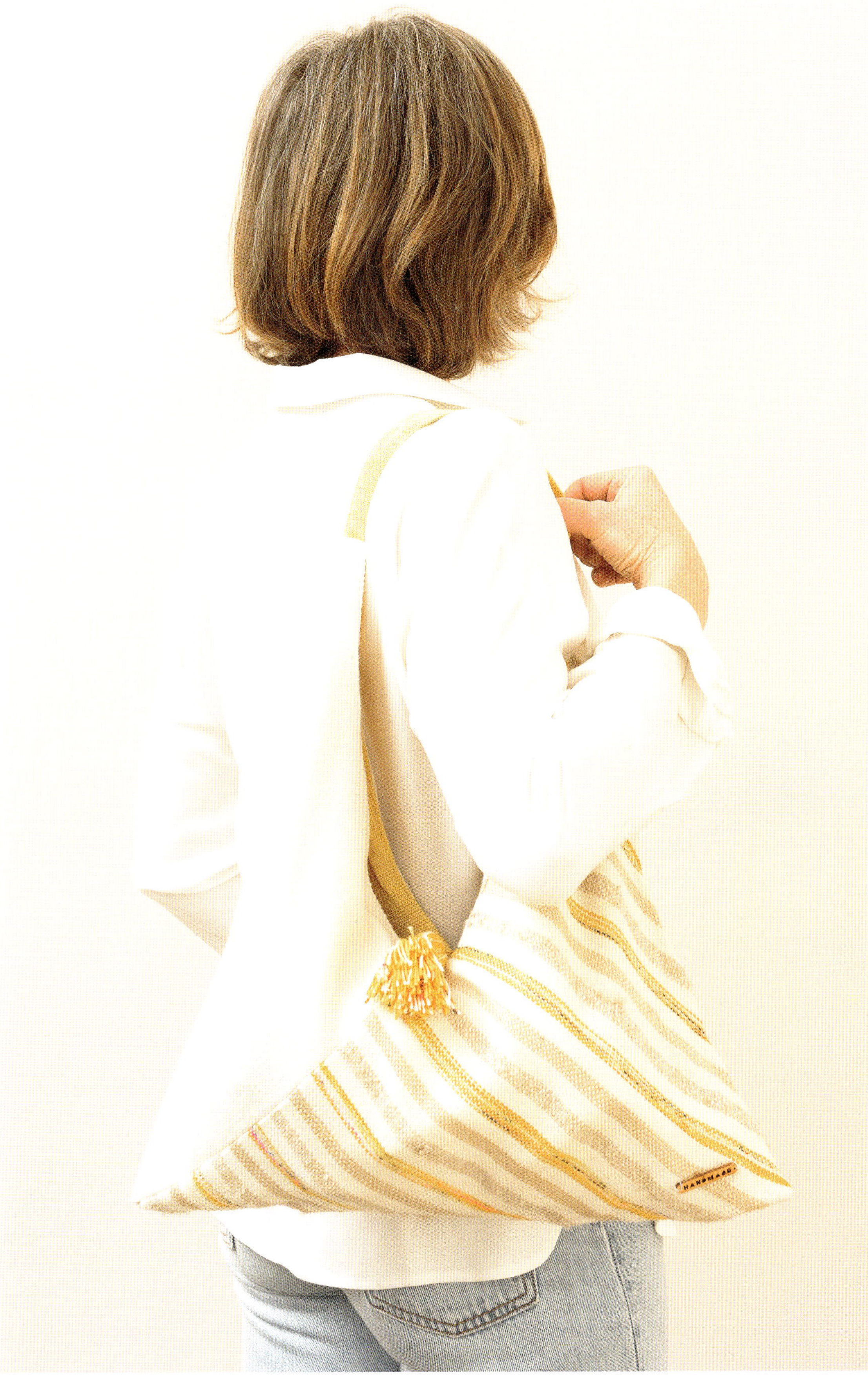
HANDMADE

Instructions

1 Wind on a warp 14 inches wide by 1½ yards long (35 × 140 cm) with the Yaku yarn in Rahvid, using a 12.5-dent (50/10) heddle. Carefully center your warp on the loom.

2 After evening out the warp with thick cotton yarn, prepare 4 shuttles with the different weft yarns.

3 Work about 14 inches (36 cm) of plain weave with the CaMaRose Rahvid.

4 Weave the stripes. Alternate about ½ inch (1.5 cm) in Rahvid and ½ inch (1.5 cm) in one of the 3 remaining colors for 28 inches (71 cm). Your fabric is now 42 inches (107 cm) long.

5 Cut your piece from the loom at the top, leaving 4 inches (10 cm) of thread and tie temporary knots to secure the weave.

6 Unwind your weave from the front beam. Untie the knots at the beginning and remove the thick cotton yarn used to even out the warp.

7 Secure both ends with a zigzag stitch on the sewing machine or stitch over with a serger.

8 Wash the fabric, dry flat, and iron gently.

9 Cut out a rectangle from the lining fabric that matches the size of your woven rectangle. Sew the lining to the woven fabric on three sides with right sides together. Turn the fabric right side out using the open side, then sew it closed by hand.

10 Fold the fabric as shown in the diagram below and sew together the diagonals formed by the triangular sections on each side of the bag.

11 To form the strap or handle, simply sew the two ends together. This is the classic origami bag. Alternatively, use a strip of leftover fabric and sew it between two ends to make the bag longer and easier to carry.

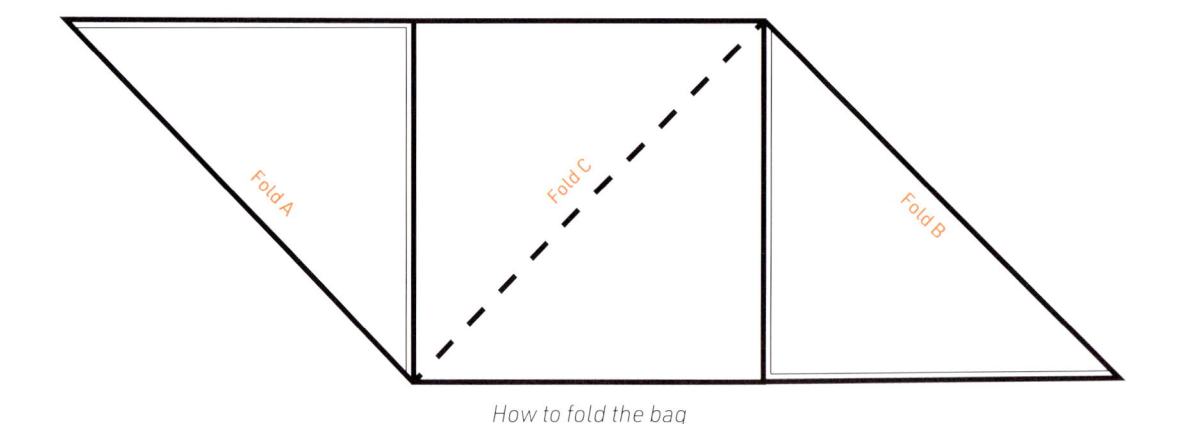

How to fold the bag

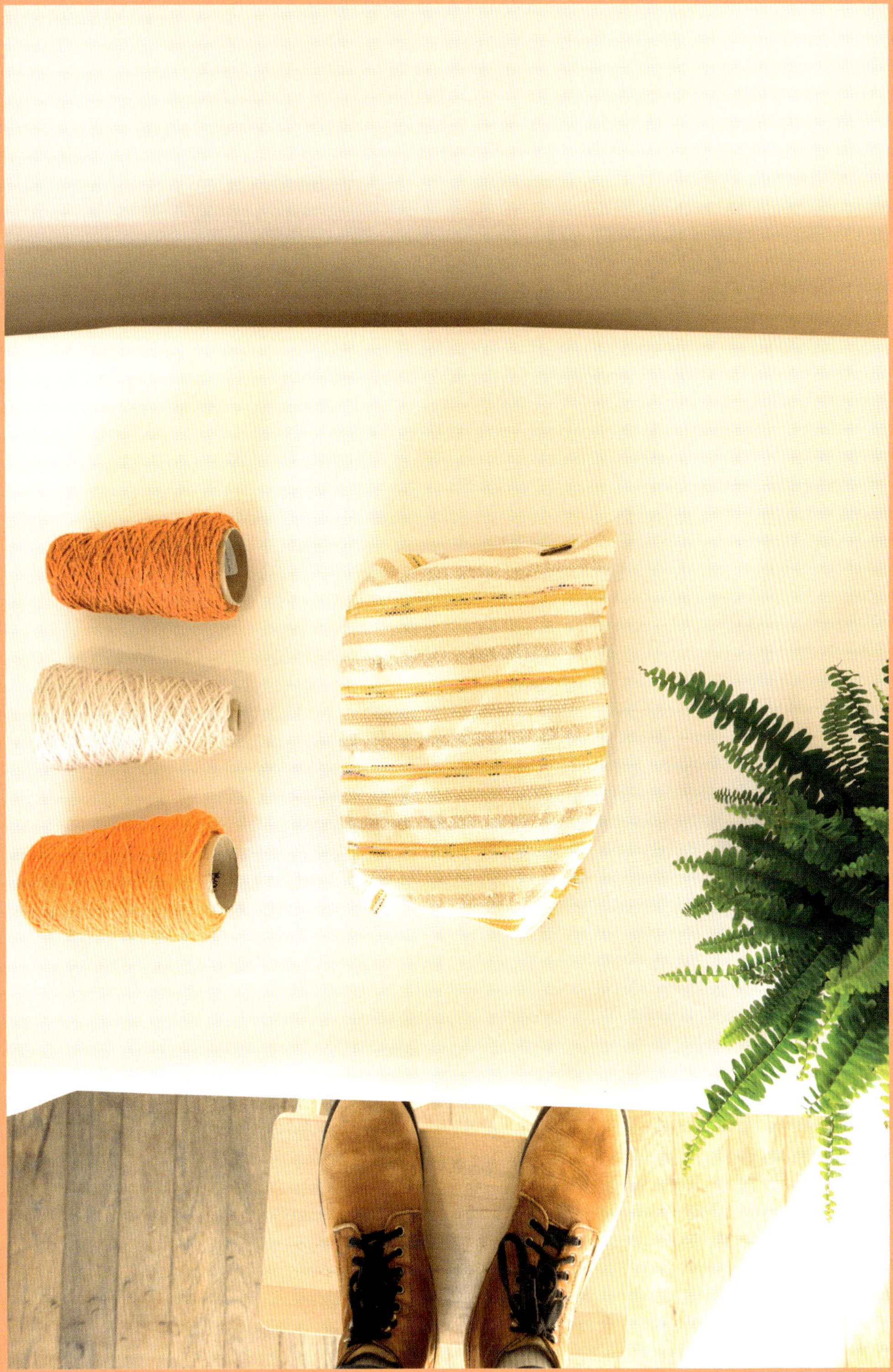

Clasped Weft Zippered Pouch

I find the effects of clasped weft beautiful and all the more graphic when you combine a solid color wool with a hand-dyed speckled wool, as in the case of this little zippered pouch. You can never have enough pouches, can you?

Techniques: Clasped weft (page 56)
Sett: 12.5 ends per inch (5 threads/cm)
Warping dimensions: 12 in. × 43 in. (30 × 110 cm) for both sides of the pouch
Final pouch dimensions: 11 in. × 6½ in. (28 × 17 cm) after sewing

Difficulty: Beginner
Time required: 5 hours
Sewing: Yes, with sewing machine

Tools and Materials
- Loom + warping materials (page 24)
- Shuttle
- Needle
- Lining fabric
- Zipper
- Sewing machine

Yarn
- Warp: CaMaRose Yaku, 2 skeins of Rahvid
- Weft:
  - Dominant color: CaMaRose Økologisk Hverdagsuld, 2 skeins Kit
  - Contrasting color: Hedgehog Fibres Sock Yarn, 1 skein Fool's Gold

Notes
- I recommend using a sewing machine.
- Pay close attention to the selvedges. This technique tends to pull a lot on the edge threads.

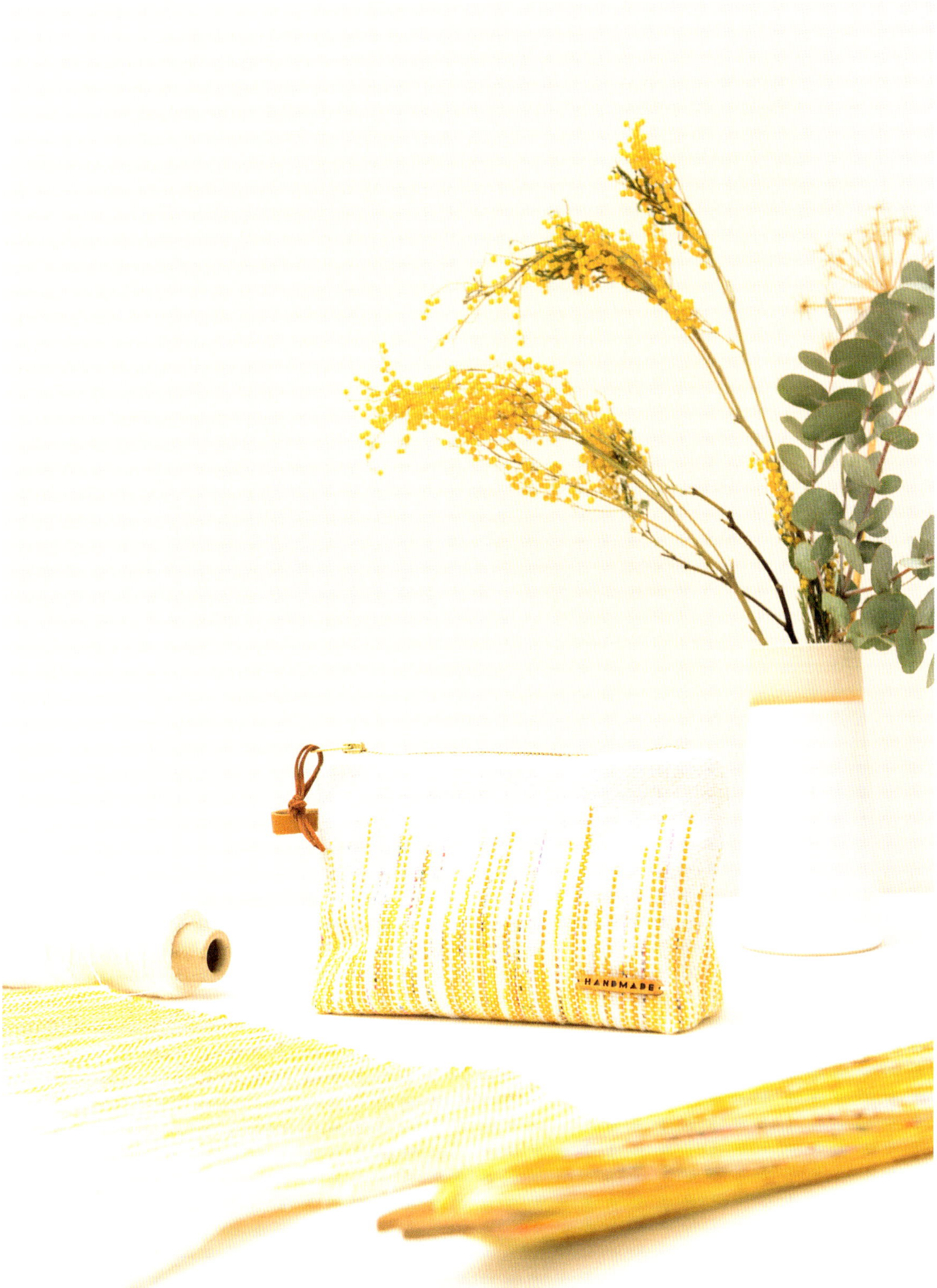
HANDMADE

Instructions

Weaving

1 Wind on a warp 12 inches wide by 43 inches long (30 × 110 cm) with the Yaku Rahvid, using a 12.5-dent (50/10) heddle. Carefully center your warp on the loom.

2 After evening out the warp with thick cotton yarn, prepare a shuttle with the Kit colorway. Leave the speckled wool in a bowl to the left of your loom.

3 Weave about ⅜ in. (1 cm) in plain weave with the Kit colorway for the seam allowance.

4 Start working on the clasped weft. Always pass your shuttle from right to left in the shed. Take it out to the left, wrap the ball of speckled wool around it and reinsert the shuttle into the shed from left to right pulling the speckled wool. Position the two yarns as desired, creating random peaks. Change the position of the heddle and start again.

5 Continue in this manner for at least 27½ inches (70 cm) in length, always varying the position of the peaks to create an interesting pattern.

6 Weave about ⅜ inch (1 cm) in plain weave with the Kit colorway for the seam allowance.

7 Cut your piece from the loom at the top, leaving 4 inches (10 cm) of thread and tie temporary knots to keep it from unraveling while being moved.

8 Unwind your weave from the front beam. Untie the knots at the beginning and remove the thick cotton yarn used to even out the warp.

9 Cut the fabric in the middle and secure both edges with a zigzag stitch on the sewing machine or sew the edges with a serger.

10 Wash the woven fabric, dry flat, and iron if needed.

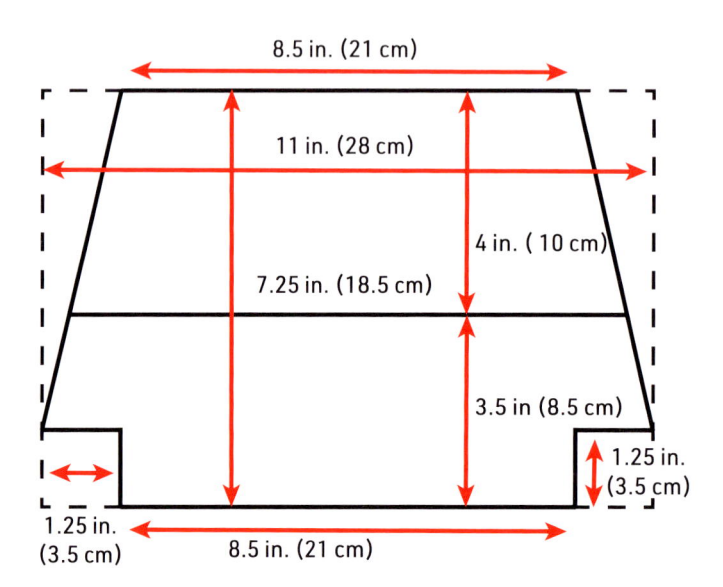

Template of the pouch and its lining

108 - Complete Guide to Rigid Heddle Weaving

Sewing the Pouch

11 On page 108 you'll find the template for the pouch. Cut 2 pieces from your woven fabric and 2 pieces from the lining.

12 Pin the zipper to one of the woven pieces, right sides together, aligning the raw edges, and pin the lining on top, wrong side facing you.

Seam
Woven fabric 1 (right side)
Lining 1 (wrong side)

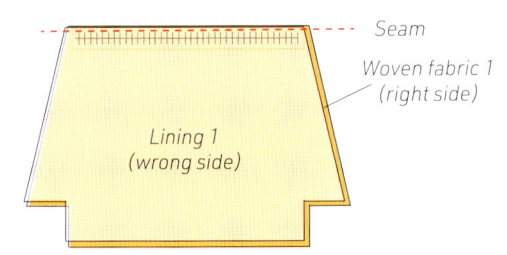

13 Sew in straight stitch, using a special zipper foot, sewing as close as possible to the zipper teeth.

14 Open the zipper and press the seams.

15 Pin the other side of the zipper to the second woven piece, right sides together. Pin the piece of lining on top (wrong side facing you).

Seam
Woven fabric 2 (right side)
Lining 2 (wrong side)
Lining + woven piece already sewn together

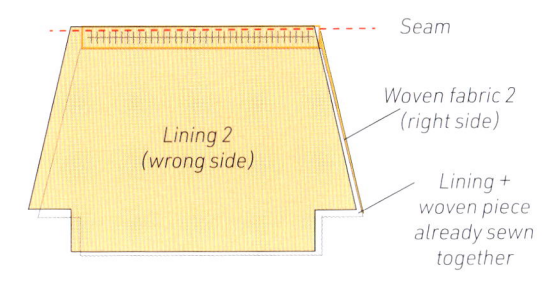

16 Sew again, using the special zipper foot close to the teeth.

17 Open the zipper and press the seams.

18 Place the two woven pieces with right sides together and the lining pieces with right sides together.

Sew in straight stitch all the way around the project, leaving an opening of about 2½ inches (6 cm) at the bottom of the lining fabric.

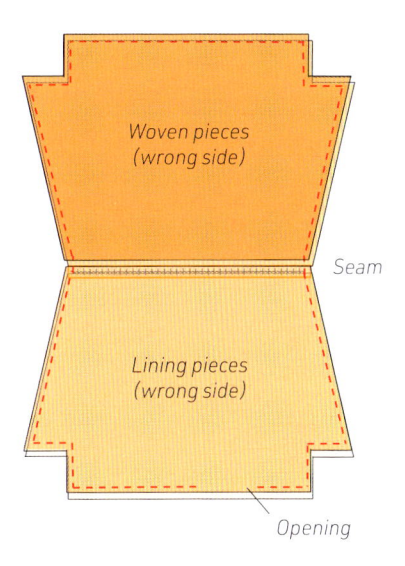

Woven pieces (wrong side)
Seam
Lining pieces (wrong side)
Opening

19 Turn the pouch right side out through the opening left in the lining. Push out the corners with a pointed tool, then close the opening in the seam by hand stitching with the invisible stitch.

Clasped Weft Zippered Pouch - 109

Pair of Dish Towels

Contrary to appearances, houndstooth and its variants are among the easiest patterns to produce on the rigid heddle loom. It is a plain weave, and the effects are achieved solely by how the two colors are distributed in the warp.

For these dish towels, three different patterns are warped in width, each separated by a strip. As for the length, there are six variations. So, these matching tea towels offer you a real array of patterns and a chance to experiment with different combinations.

Techniques: Color effects (page 54)
Sett: 12.5 ends per inch (5 threads/cm)
Warping dimensions: 18 in. × 6½ ft. (46 × 200 cm)
Final dimensions of towels: 2 towels 16 in. × 23 in. (40 × 58 cm) each

Difficulty: Intermediate
Time required: 6 hours
Sewing: Hem, can do by hand

Tools and Materials
- Loom + warping materials (page 24)
- 3 shuttles
- Needle
- 2 small strips of cotton 2¼ in. × ⅜ in. (6 × 1 cm)

Yarn
Sandnes Garn Mandarin Petit
- Warp:
  - 1½ skeins White
  - 1½ skeins Chili
  - 1 skein Sandstein
- Weft:
  - 1½ skeins White
  - 1½ skeins Chili
  - 1 skein Sandstein

Notes

- It is best to use the same yarn in warp and weft, preferably in highly contrasting colors. Otherwise, the pattern will not show as well.
- I find that hand stitching the hems with an invisible stitch is better and cleaner, but you can sew them with a sewing machine or a serger if you prefer.
- There are six variations in these two dish towels.

1. Weave only with White.
2. Weave only with Chili.
3. Weave only with Sandstein.
4. Alternate 1 row White and 1 row Chili.
5. Alternate 2 rows White and 2 rows Chili.
6. Alternate 4 rows White and 4 rows Chili.

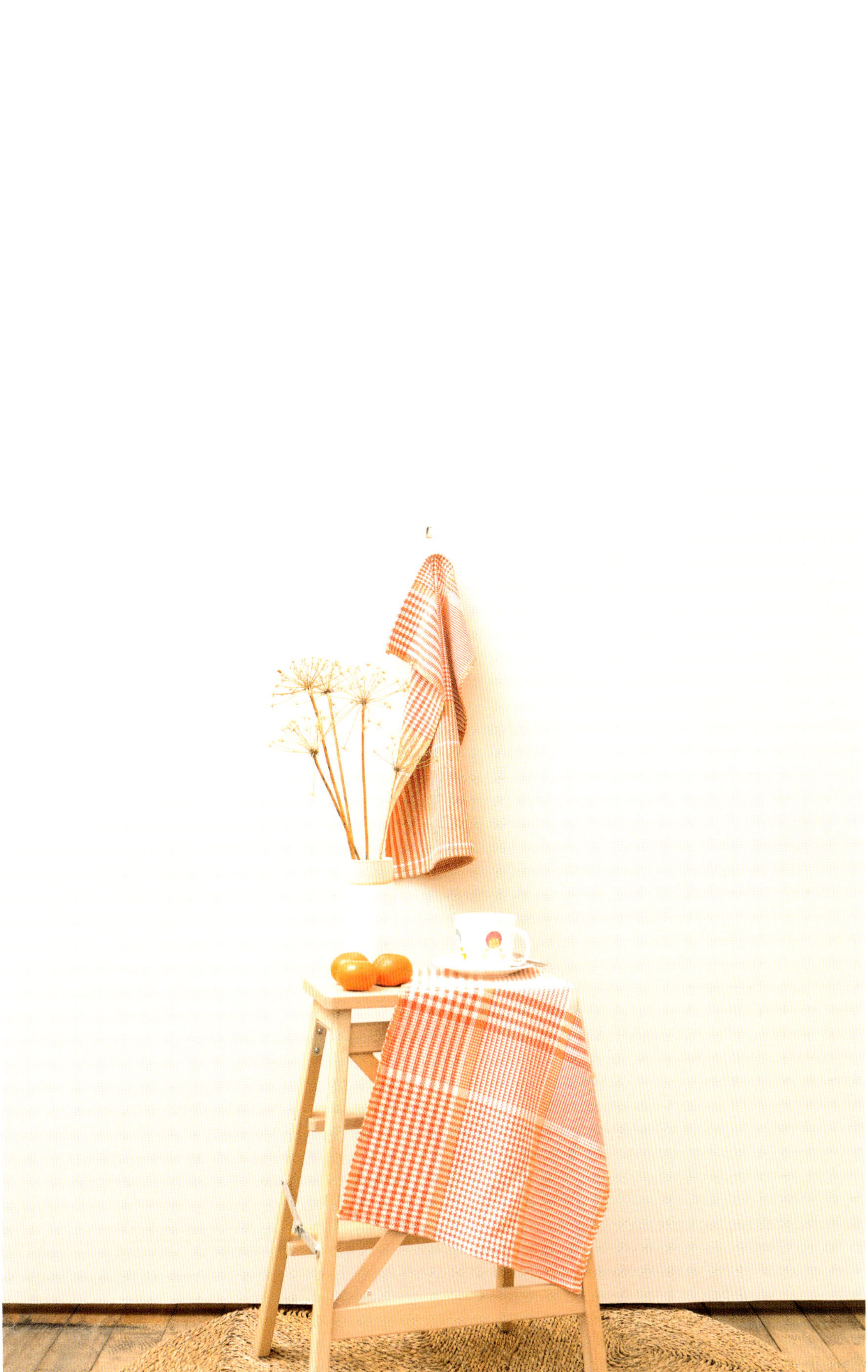

Instructions

Warping

1 Thread the slots: Direct warp the 6½ ft. long by 1½ ft. wide (2 m × 46 cm) warp through the 12.5-dent (50/10) heddle, as follows.

- Tie the Sandstein yarn onto the back bar and use it to thread 5 slots.
- Tie the White and Chili yarns around the back bar and thread 32 slots, always alternating 1 slot in White and 1 in Chili.
- Repeat these two steps once more.
- Tie the Sandstein color yarn onto the back bar and use it to thread 5 slots.
- Tie the White and Chili yarn around the back bar and thread 32 slots, still alternating colors, this time 2 slots in White and 2 in Chili.
- Tie the Sandstein yarn onto the back bar and use it to thread 5 slots.

Good to Know

Only cut and retie the Sandstein yarn.
The White and Chili yarns can cross behind the heddle without affecting the weave.

---

2 Thread the eyes: To thread the eyes you'll need to do a little sleight-of-hand for the first pattern on the right in order to warp three different patterns

- **4 stripes of Sandstein only.** Thread as usual: the right-hand thread in the right-hand eye, while the left-hand thread remains in the slot.
- **Right pattern: 1 White thread, 1 Chili thread.** Place all White threads in the eyes and all Chili threads in the slots. To do this, you'll need to pull some threads out of the heddle.
- **Middle pattern: 2 White threads, 2 Chili threads.** Thread as usual: the right-hand thread in the right-hand eye while the left-hand thread remains in the slot.
- **Left pattern: 4 White threads, 4 Chili threads.** Thread as usual: right-hand thread in right-hand eye while the left-hand thread remains in the slot.

3 After evening out the warp with a thick cotton yarn, prepare 3 shuttles with the different yarns.

4 Work the first 4 rows in plain weave with Sandstein.

Hemstitch

If you want to do a hemstitch (see page 43), leave a tail at least 32 inches (80 cm) at the beginning of the weave and, in step 4, thread a needle to complete the stitch.

You will now weave the dish towels one after the other from this warp.

Dish Towel 1

5 Weave, alternating the yarn as follows:

- 2 inches (5 cm) in Sandstein
- 2 rows in White
- 7 inches (18 cm) in Sandstein
- 2 rows in White
- 3 inches (8 cm) in Sandstein
- 2⅜ inches (6 cm) alternating 2 rows in Chili and 2 rows in White (the houndstooth pattern should appear in the middle of the three stripes)
- 4 rows in Sandstein
- 5 inches (13 cm) alternating 1 row in White and 1 row in Chili
- ¾ inch (2 cm) in White
- 2¾ inches (7 cm) alternating 2 rows in Chili and 2 rows in White (the houndstooth pattern should appear in the middle of the three stripes).

This is the end of the first dish towel.

Hemstitch

If you want to do a hemstitch, do so at this point to secure the first dish towel.

6 Weave a strip at least 1¼ inches (3 cm) with the White yarn; this will allow you to cut apart the two dish towels when the weave is finished.

Dish Towel 2

Hemstitch

If you want to do a hemstitch, do so at this point to secure the second dish towel.

7 Weave, alternating the yarn as follows:
- 6 rows in White
- 3 inches (8 cm), alternating 1 row in White and 1 row in Chili
- 6 rows in Chili
- 1½ inches (4 cm), alternating 4 rows in Chili and 4 rows in White
- 6 rows in Chili
- 5 inches (13 cm) in Chili
- 2 rows in Sandstein
- 3 inches (8 cm) in White.

The second dish towel ends here, with a final row from left to right.

Hemstitch

If you'd like to do a hemstitch, leave a length of at least 32 inches (80 cm) at the end of weaving, then thread it through a needle to complete the stitch.

Separating and Finishing the Dish Towels

8 Cut your weave from the loom at the top, leaving 1¼ inches (3 cm) if you've opted for the hemstitch. Otherwise, leave 2 to 2¼ inches (5-6 cm) of thread before tying temporary knots to secure the weave while it is being moved.

9 Unwind your weave from the front beam. Untie the knots at the beginning and remove the thick cotton yarn used to even out the warp.

10 Separate the two towels by cutting down the middle of the center white strip.

Pair of Dish Towels - 113

11 If you did not do a hemstitch, sew a zigzag stitch on both ends of the dish towels.

12 Wash both towels in hot water, dry flat, and iron.

13 Double hem both ends of each dish towel. On the first end of the dish towel, fold over ⅜ inch (1 cm) toward the back side and iron the fold. Fold the same edge toward the back again about ⅜ inch (1 cm), and iron. Place a strip of cotton or similar, folded in half, at the end of the hem, so that it is caught in the seam and allows you to hang the dish towel when finished (see photo below). Pin the hem along its entire length before sewing. Repeat on the other end.

14 Iron both dish towels, especially the hems.

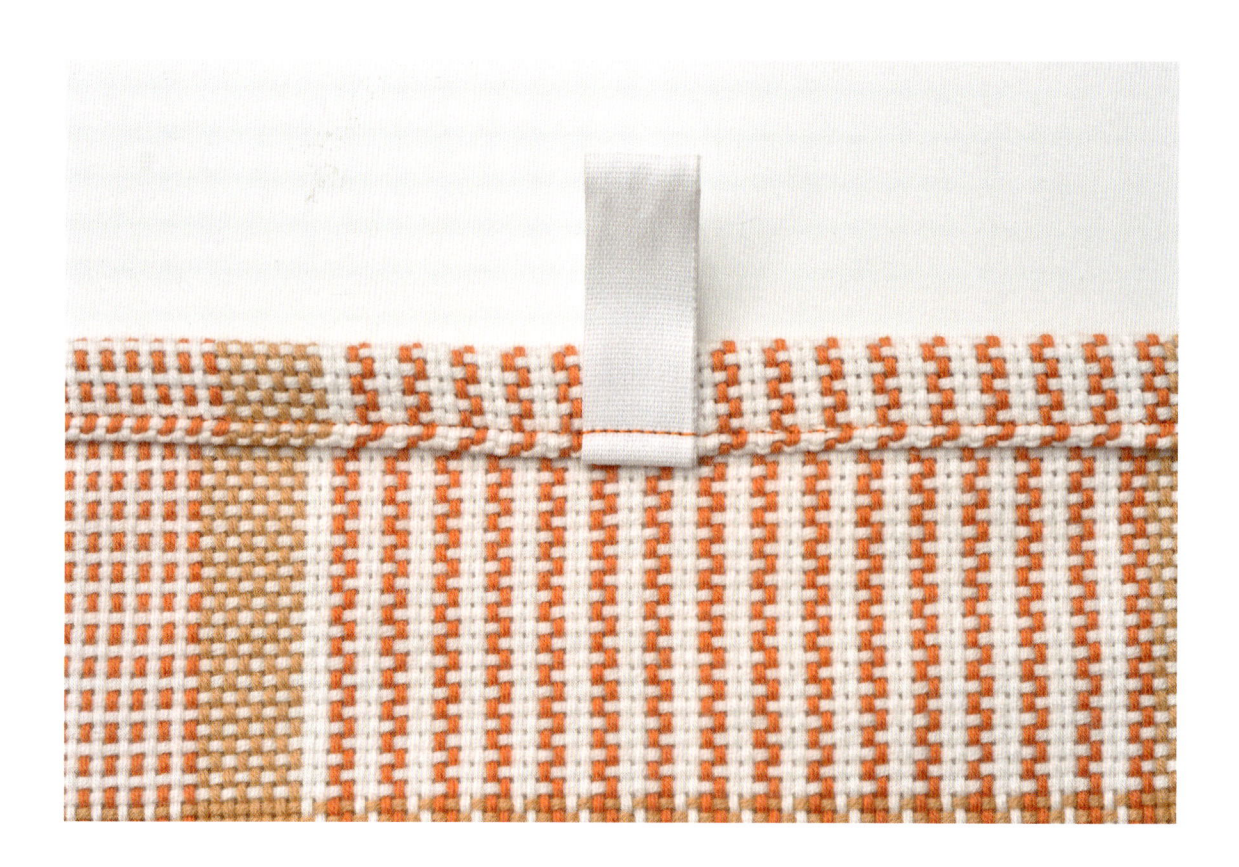

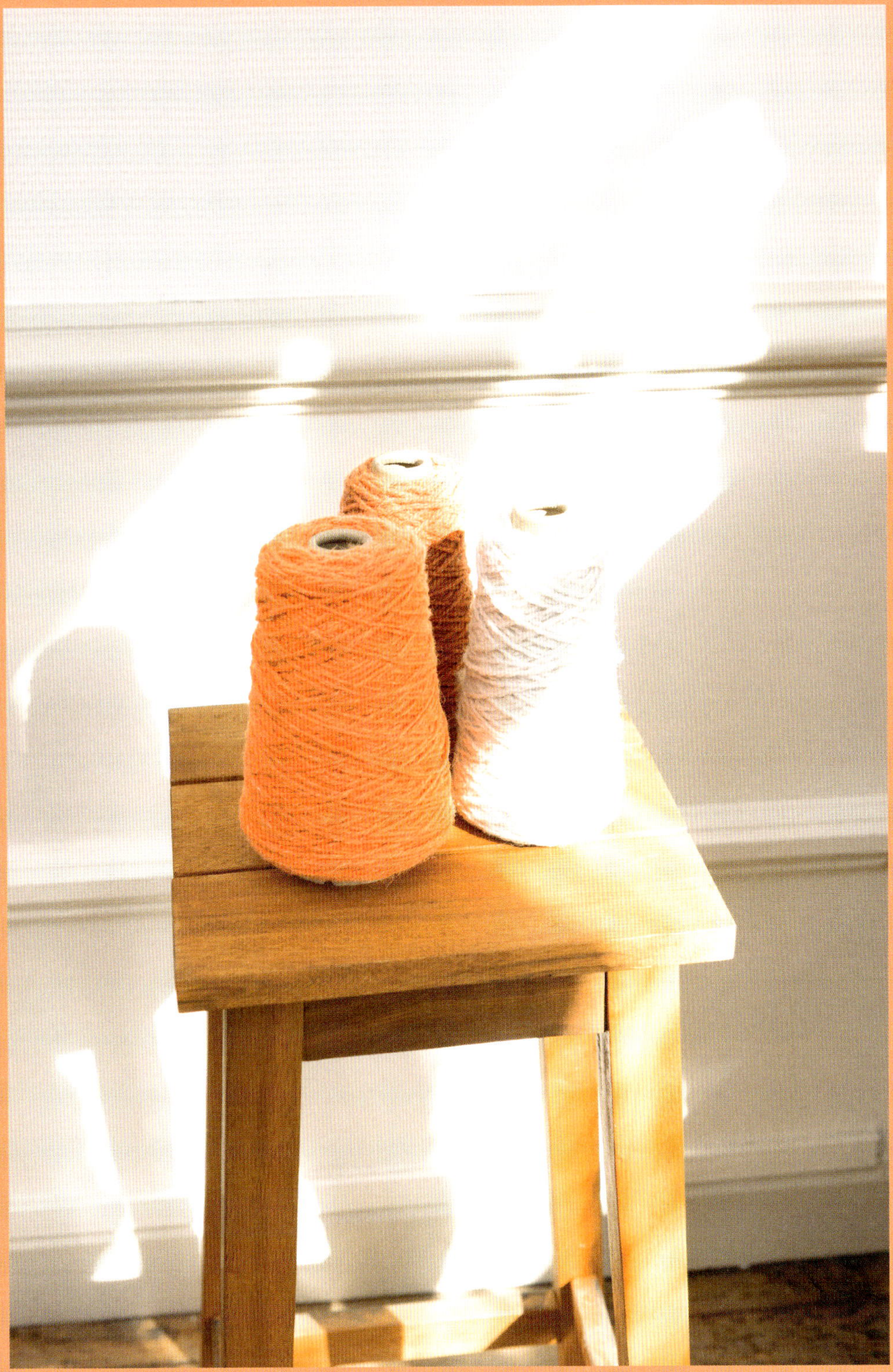

Saori Wall Hanging

This is a fun and relaxing project, if you can put your perfectionism aside for a few hours. Saori is a Japanese technique that lets you unleash your creativity and have fun with as many different materials as possible, without worrying too much about symmetry or consistency. On the contrary! Here we're looking for something more organic and spontaneous.

Techniques: Saori (page 60)
Sett: 10 ends per inch (4 threads/cm)
Warping dimensions: 18 in. × 60 in. (45 × 150 cm)
Final dimensions of the piece: about 16 in. × 40 in. (40 × 100 cm), including fringe and wood

Difficulty: Beginner
Time required: 6 hours
Sewing: No

Tools and Materials
- Loom + warping materials (page 24)
- 3 or 4 shuttles
- Needle
- Driftwood for hanging

Yarn
- Warp: Phildar Phil Coton 3, 2 balls in Black
- Weft: various yarns and fibers from Funem
  - Merino wool roving in Camel, Powder, and Beige
  - Natural cotton cord in 3/16 in. and 5/16 in. (5 and 9 mm)
  - Natural silk
  - Roll of Gray wool
  - Chunky felt cord in Ivory
  - DMC Woolly in Sand, Cream, Pigeon, and Shadow
  - Recycled Sari silk thread in Mint
  - Frizz cotton ribbon in Alcazar
  - Fine felted wool in Powder
  - Fine alpaca wool in Beige

Notes

You can incorporate all kinds of materials into this weave, so don't hold back! Think of using plant materials, pieces of paper, beads, or fabric scraps. Since this weave leaves a lot to improvisation, I haven't written down the thread quantities—trust yourself!

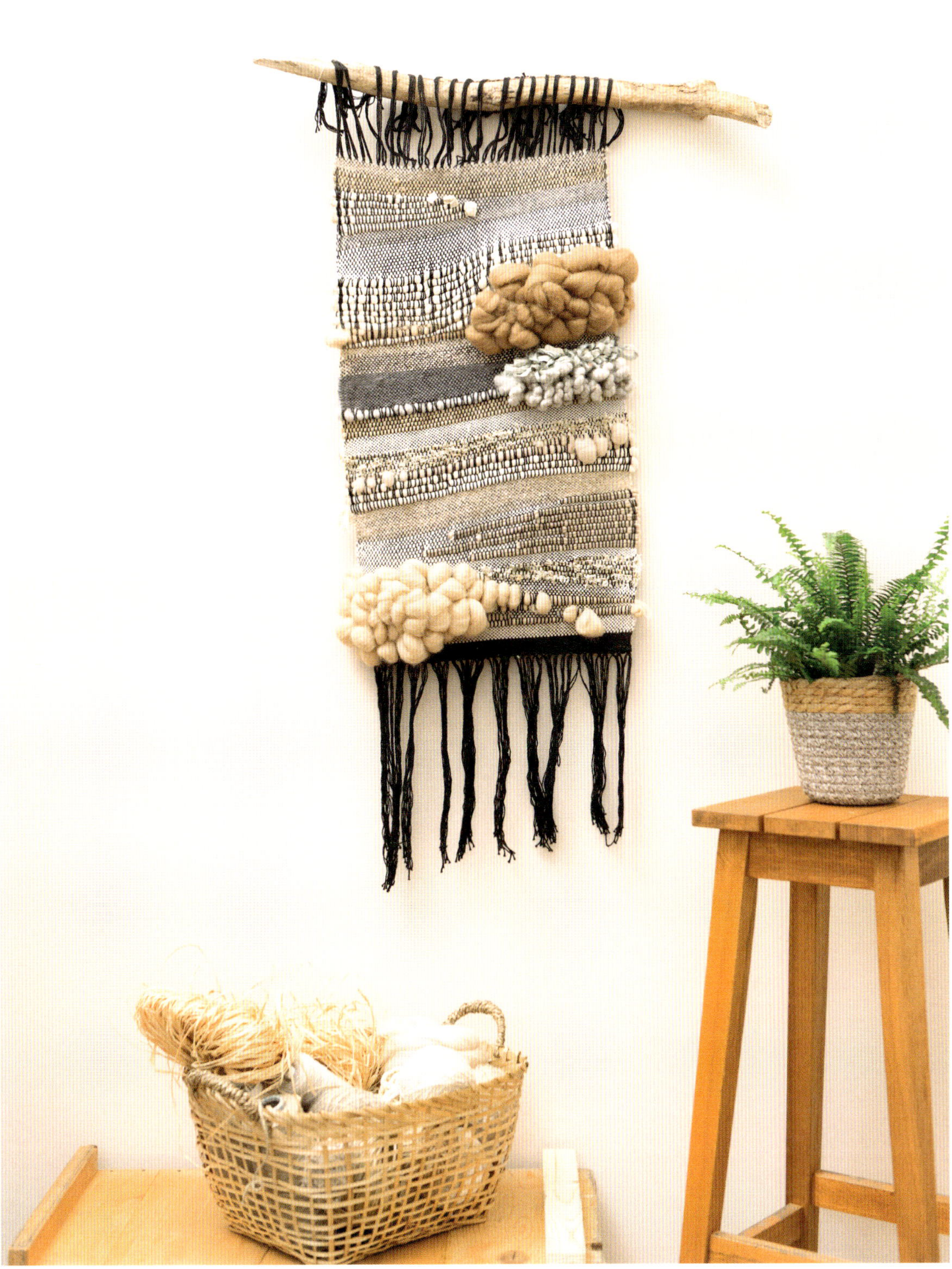

Instructions

1 Wind on a warp 18 inches wide by 5 ft. long (45 × 150 cm) with the Phil Coton Black, using a 10-dent (40/10) heddle. Carefully center your warp on the loom.

2 After evening out the warp with a thick cotton yarn, prepare one shuttle for each material.

3 Work the first 4 rows in plain weave with the Black cotton, leaving a tail of at least 32 in. (80 cm) at the beginning of the weave.

4 Thread the tail of this yarn through the needle and hemstitch (see page 43).

5 Work ¾ inch (2 cm) in plain weave with the Black cotton. Be extra careful at the selvedges and always beat the weft in from a 45-degree angle.

6 Continue with the plain weave and change the weft material as you go, making stripes two or so inches wide (several centimeters). To create the pattern shown here, follow the steps below.

- Weave around an inch (a few centimeters) with the Woolly yarn in Cream.
- Insert Powder roving wool in the next rows with your fingers to continue the weave. Pull large loops up between the warp threads on the left side to add volume.
- Weave a few rows with the Woolly yarn in Cream then make half-rows with the Frizz ribbon and follow that with the Cream Woolly yarn again.
- Weave a clasped weft pattern (see page 56) with the Woolly in Cream and the fine felted wool over several rows.
- Follow with the alpaca for an inch or so (a few centimeters) and then use the thinner cotton cord and the Beige wool roving for a few rows.
- Weave stripes with the Frizz cotton ribbon, the Cream Woolly, and the natural silk, then add a stripe with the roll of Gray wool and, on the right side of the piece, pull up large loops of this yarn between the warp threads.
- Continue with the Woolly yarn in Shadow for an inch or so (a few centimeters).
- On the right, insert a small piece of the recycled Sari silk and pull loops up on the front.
- Follow with recycled cotton and then the Woolly yarn in Beige.
- Add a strip of the wool roving in Camel and pull large loops up between the warp threads on the right-hand side of the piece.
- Continue weaving with stripes of the Chunky felt cord in Ivory, then with the thicker cotton cord, the Woolly yarn in Cream, and then Woolly Pigeon.
- Weave a few rows with the natural silk.

7 Finish with 1¼ in. (3 cm) of plain weave with the alpaca. The last row must be woven from left to right. Leave a tail of at least 32 inches (80 cm) at the end of the weave.

8 Thread the end of this alpaca through the needle and hemstitch the end.

9 Cut your weave from the loom at the top, leaving at least 8 inches (20 cm) of thread to accommodate the piece of driftwood. The hemstitch secures the weaving, so there is no need to tie knots.

10 Unwind your weaving from the front beam. Untie the knots at the beginning and remove the thick cotton used to even out the warp. Use a ruler to straighten the bottom of the fringe.

11 Iron your piece on the reverse side.

12 To finish the top, tie the warp ends around the driftwood branch so you can hang it on the wall.

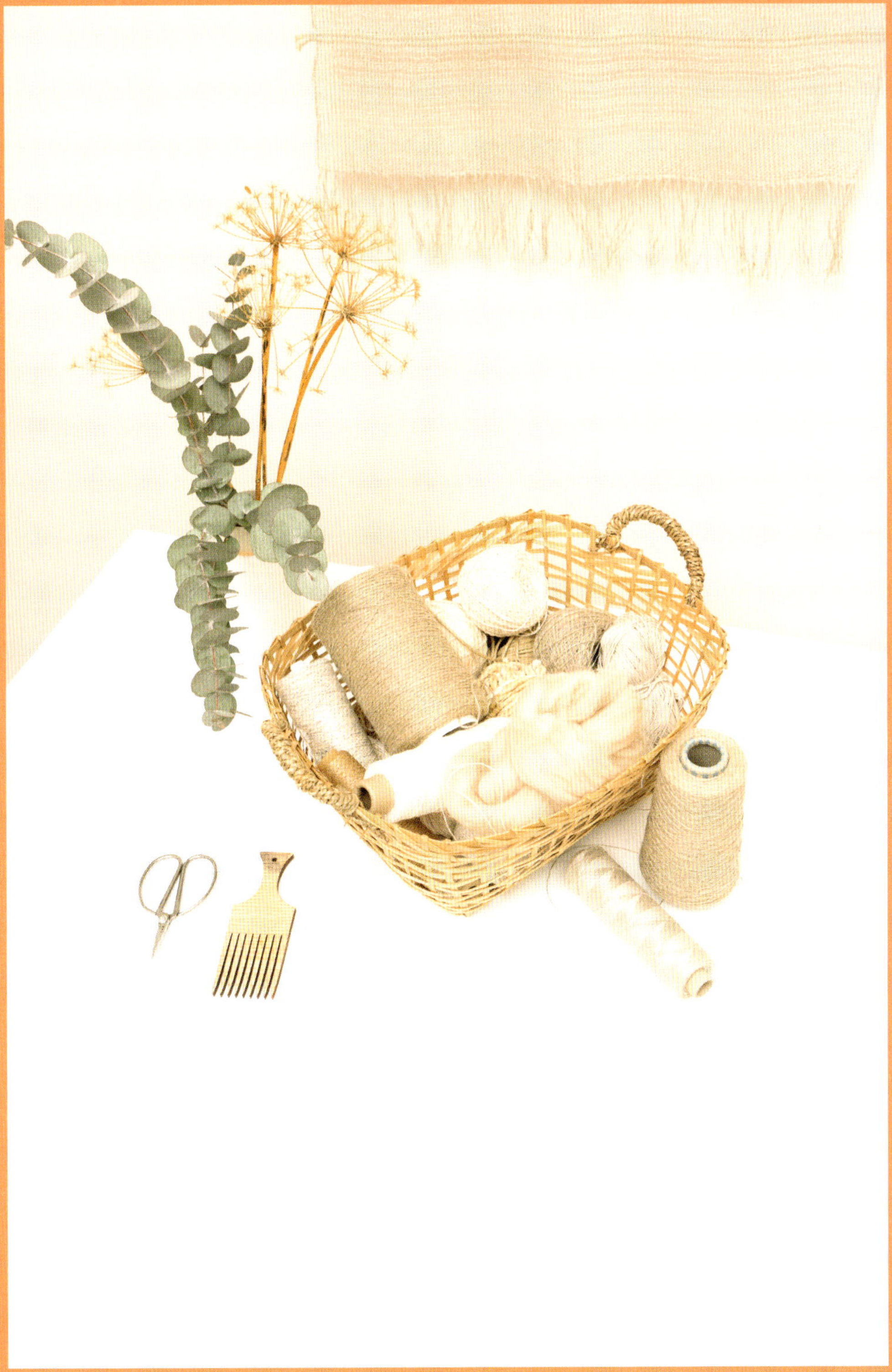

Light and Airy Wall Hanging

This wall hanging is the opposite of the previous one: light, delicate, and practically transparent. It developed from a sampler created with fibers that are unusual for me: plant fibers. It includes linen, paper, horsehair, raffia, and cotton. To accentuate the impression of fragility, I deliberately left spaces in the warp and added Danish medallions in the center to create a contrast between these rounded, organic parts and the simple linearity of the weave. The low density of the fabric highlights the natural beauty of the different fibers.

Techniques: Spaced warp (page 57) and Danish medallions (page 67)
Sett: 10 ends per inch (4 threads/cm)
Warping dimensions: 13 in. × 47 in. (33 × 120 cm)
Final dimensions of the wall hanging: 12 in. × 30 in. (30 × 75 cm), including fringe and hem

Difficulty: Intermediate
Time required: 5 hours
Sewing: Handsewn hem

Tools and Materials
- Loom + warping materials (page 24)
- 4 shuttles
- Needle
- Crochet hook
- Hair comb
- Wood stick or dowel (approx. 1 ¼ in./30 mm)

Yarn
- Warp: Alysse Creations 6/2 Linen yarn on cone, natural
- Weft: Mix of various plant fibers
  - Alysse Creations 6/2 Linen yarn on cone, natural
  - Alysse Creations 6/2 Linen yarn on cone, bleached
  - Funem recycled cotton yarn
  - ForestsAndMeadows Bouclé linen yarn
  - Raffia
  - PaperPhine paper yarn
  - Funem metallic string
  - Bart and Francis Horsehair

Notes
- The only reason I am indicating intermediate level for this wall hanging is because the warp is linen. The weaving itself is easy, but warping linen can be a real challenge due to its lack of elasticity (see page 17).
- You will need a hair comb to help you beat the weft where there is openwork.

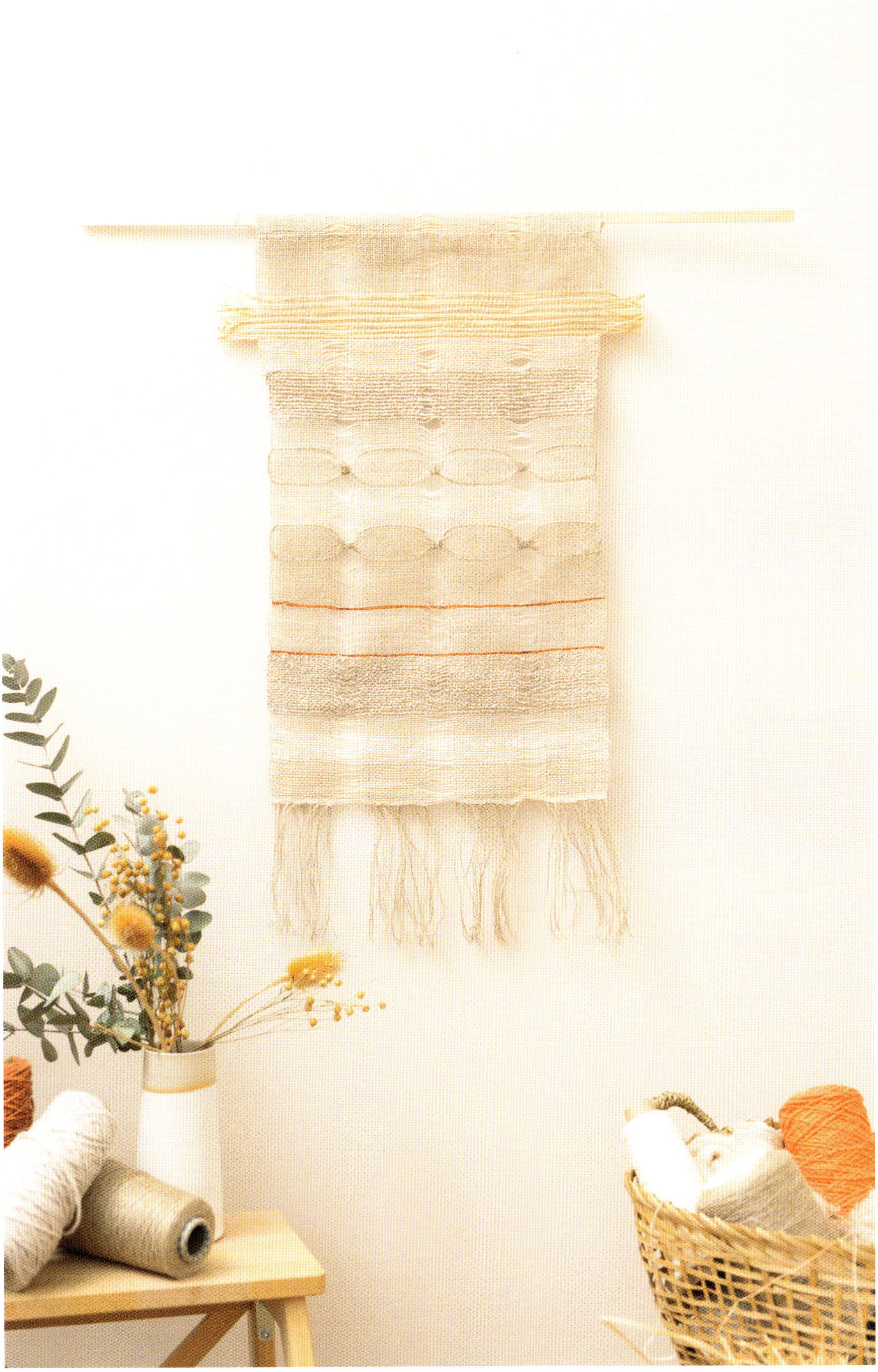

Instructions

1 Wind on a warp 13 inches wide by 47 inches long (33 × 120 cm) with the natural linen, using a 10-dent (40/10) heddle, leaving spaces in the warp as follows: *thread 16 slots, leave 6 slots empty.* Complete from * to * 3 times, then thread another 16 slots. There's no need to cut or tie the yarn before leaving slots empty. Simply skip the slots and continue on 6 slots later.

2 After evening out the warp with thick cotton yarn, prepare 1 shuttle per material.

3 Work the first 4 rows in plain weave with the natural linen, leaving a 28-in. (70 cm) tail or longer at the start of the weave.

4 Thread the end of this yarn through the needle and hemstitch (see page 43).

5 Work in plain weave and change materials as you go along, making plain weave stripes a couple of inches (several centimeters) long. To make the pattern shown here, use the shuttles in this order:

- natural linen yarn
- paper yarn
- horsehair
- bouclé linen yarn
- metallic yarn
- horsehair
- metallic yarn
- natural linen yarn

6 Toward the middle of the piece, add two rows of Danish medallions using a crochet hook, separated by a stripe about 2 inches (5 cm) high woven with paper yarn.

Use a double thickness of the linen yarn for the outline around the medallions. For the width of the medallions, take all the warp threads up to the spaces left by the 6 empty slots. Make several loops, repeating step 9 for making medallions (see page 67) to make them stand out well.

7 Continue weaving several stripes in plain weave until the piece is 27 to 28 inches (70 cm) long. You may wish to alternate the yarns as follows:

- natural linen yarn
- recycled cotton
- bleached linen yarn
- raffia
- natural linen yarn

8 Finish with 2 inches (5 cm) of bleached linen and leave a tail of at least 27 inches (70 cm) at the end of the weave. Weave the last row from left to right and thread the tail through the needle to hemstitch the end.

9 Cut your weave from the loom at the top, leaving about 2 inches (5 cm) of thread after the hemstitch. Since the hemstitch secures the weave, there is no need to knot the warp ends.

10 Unwind your weaving from the front beam. Untie the knots at the beginning and remove the thick cotton used to even out the warp. Use a ruler to straighten the bottom of the fringe.

11 Cut the remaining threads at the top, leaving a little over an inch (3 cm).

12 Iron your piece with a hot iron on the reverse side.

13 To finish the top, make a double hem. Fold the edge of the fabric ⅜ inch (1 cm) toward the back side and iron the fold. Fold the same edge toward the back again about an inch or more (3 cm), and iron. Pin the hem along its entire length and sew by hand, working an invisible stitch with the linen yarn. The threads remaining at the top of the weave are folded into the hem. Insert the wood dowel into the space created by the hem so you can hang it.

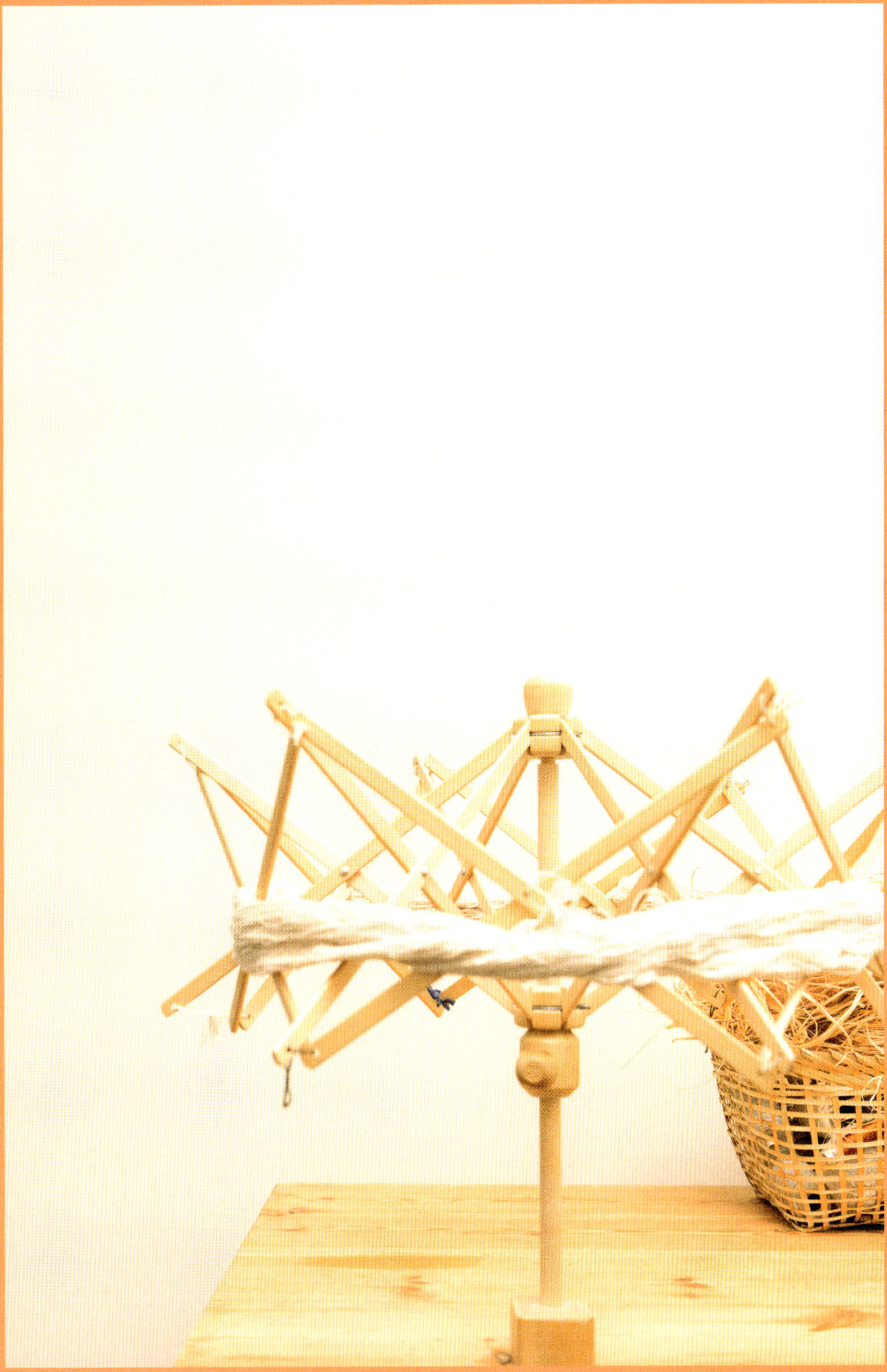

Café Curtain

Want to have some fun with openwork stitches? This is the project for you! This little linen café curtain is surprisingly quick to make. You can, of course, vary the openwork stitches or remove the cord if you prefer.

Openwork techniques: Leno (page 62) and brooks bouquet (page 65)
Sett: 10 ends per inch (4 threads/cm)
Warping dimensions: 25½ in. × 47 in. (65 × 120 cm)
Final dimensions of curtain: 23½ in. × 27½ in. (60 × 70 cm), including fringe and hem

> Difficulty: Intermediate
> Time required: 8 hours
> Sewing: Handsewn hem

Tools and Materials
- Loom + warping materials (page 24)
- 2 shuttles
- Needle
- Hair comb
- Pick-up stick
- Wood dowel or stick slightly wider than your weave for hanging

Yarn
- Warp: Alysse Creations 6/2 Linen yarn on cone, natural
- Weft:
    - Alysse Creations 6/2 Linen yarn on cone, natural
    - Cord, natural

Notes
- The use of linen in warp can be a challenge due to its lack of elasticity (see page 17). If you're just starting out, you can replace it with cotton.
- I've chosen a very low sett for this café curtain, so the openwork is really wide open. This also makes it easier to work these lacy stitches.
- You will need a hair comb to help you beat the weft where there are openwork stitches.

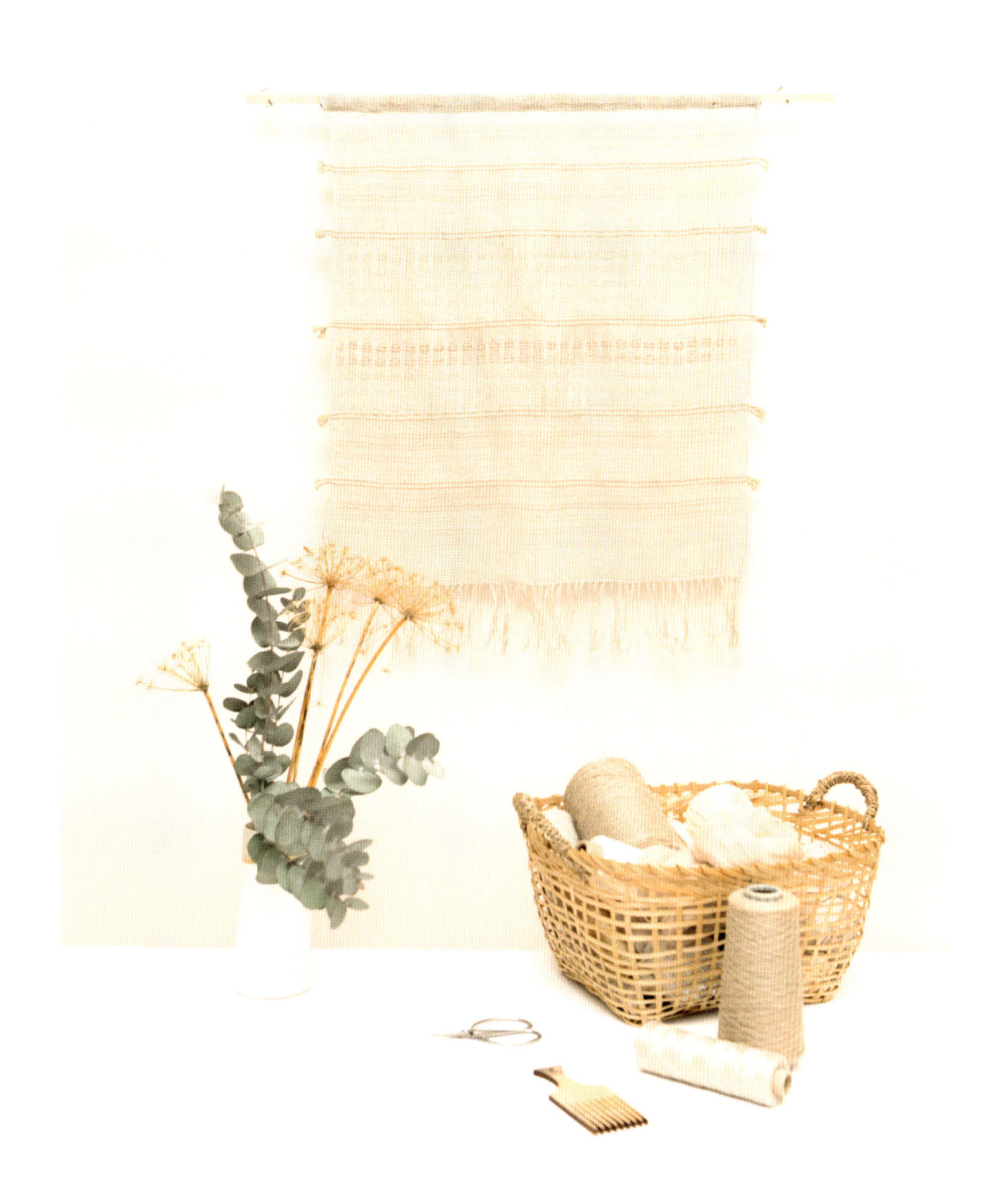

Instructions

1 Wind on a linen warp 25½ inches wide by 47 inches long (65 × 120 cm), using a 10-dent (40/10) heddle. Carefully center your warp on the loom.

2 After evening out the warp with thick cotton yarn, prepare 1 shuttle per material.

3 Work the first 4 rows in plain weave with linen, leaving about a 40-in. (100 cm) tail at the start of the weave.

4 Thread the end of this yarn through the needle and hemstitch (see page 43).

5 Continue in plain weave with linen for 2 inches (5 cm) to create the bottom border.

6 Using your pick-up stick, *start to weave the row from right to left with the leno technique to make openwork lace stitches and then follow that with 3 rows of plain weave*. Repeat from * to * 4 more times.

7 Weave back and forth in plain weave with the cord, leaving the ends extended beyond the warp on both sides.

8 Repeat steps 6 and 7 1 more time.

9 With your pick-up stick, *start weaving the row from right to left using the brooks bouquet technique for openwork stitches and follow with 5 rows of plain weave*. Repeat from * to * 4 more times.

10 Weave 5 more rows in plain weave.

11 Weave back and forth in plain weave with the cord, leaving the ends extended beyond the warp on both sides.

Good to Know

You're now halfway through your curtain; the rows will now be repeated in mirror image.

12 Work 10 rows in plain weave, then repeat steps 9 and 11, steps 6 and 7, and finish off by completing step 6 one last time.

13 Finish by working 2 inches (5 cm) of plain weave with linen (this will be the top of the curtain), leaving a tail of at least 40 inches (100 cm) at the end of the weave. Weave the last row from left to right and thread the tail through the needle to hemstitch the end.

14 Cut your weave from the loom at the top, leaving about 2 inches (5 cm) of thread after the hemstitch. Since the hemstitch secures the weave, there is no need to knot the warp ends.

15 Unwind your café curtain from the front beam. Untie the knots at the beginning and remove the thick cotton used to even out the warp. Use a ruler to straighten the fringe at the bottom, leaving about 3 to 4 inches (7.5 to 10 cm cm).

16 Wash your weave in hot water, lay flat to dry, and iron.

17 To finish the top, make a double hem. Fold the edge of the fabric ⅜ inch (1 cm) toward the back side and iron the fold. Fold the same edge toward the back again about an inch or more (3 cm), and iron. Pin the hem along its entire length and sew by hand, working an invisible stitch with the linen yarn. The threads remaining at the top of the weave are folded into the hem. Insert a wood dowel or stick into the space created by the hem so you can hang it.

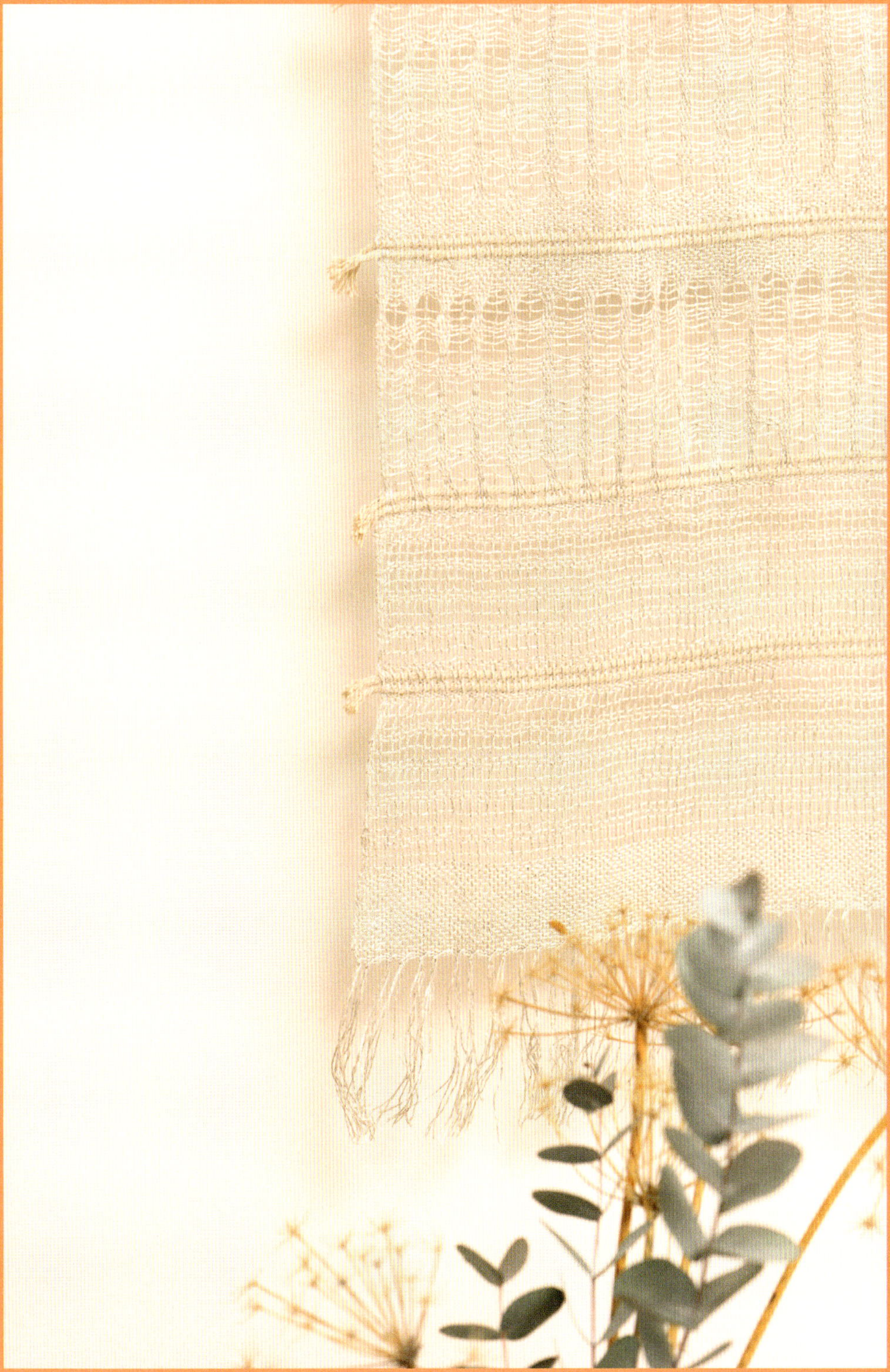

Textured Pillow

Looking for a soft, plush cushion for your sofa? This project plays with three different textured stitches to create an interesting and soft surface. It takes a little time to complete, but I find the process very relaxing, almost meditative. So arm yourself with a little patience and create a centerpiece for your home decor.

Techniques for adding texture: Soumak stitch (page 70), Rya knot (page 72), loops (page 73)
Sett: 12.5 ends per inch (5 threads/cm)
Warping dimensions: 20 in. × 31.5 in. (50 × 80 cm)
Final dimensions of pillow: 18 in. × 16 in. (45 × 40 cm)

Difficulty: Intermediate
Time required: 15 hours
Sewing: Yes, preferably with a machine

Tools and Materials
- Loom + warping materials (page 24)
- 4 shuttles
- Straight knitting needle or other round tool the width of the fabric
- Needle
- Sewing machine
- Fabric for the back of the pillow
- 16 in. × 16 in pillow insert

Yarn
- Warp: CaMaRose Yaku, 2 skeins Rahvid
- Weft:
  - CaMaRose Økologisk Hverdagsuld, 2 skeins Rahvid
  - DMC Woolly
    · 1 ball Sand
    · 1 ball Cream
    · 1 ball Pigeon
    · 1 ball Sulphur
    · 1 ball Shadow

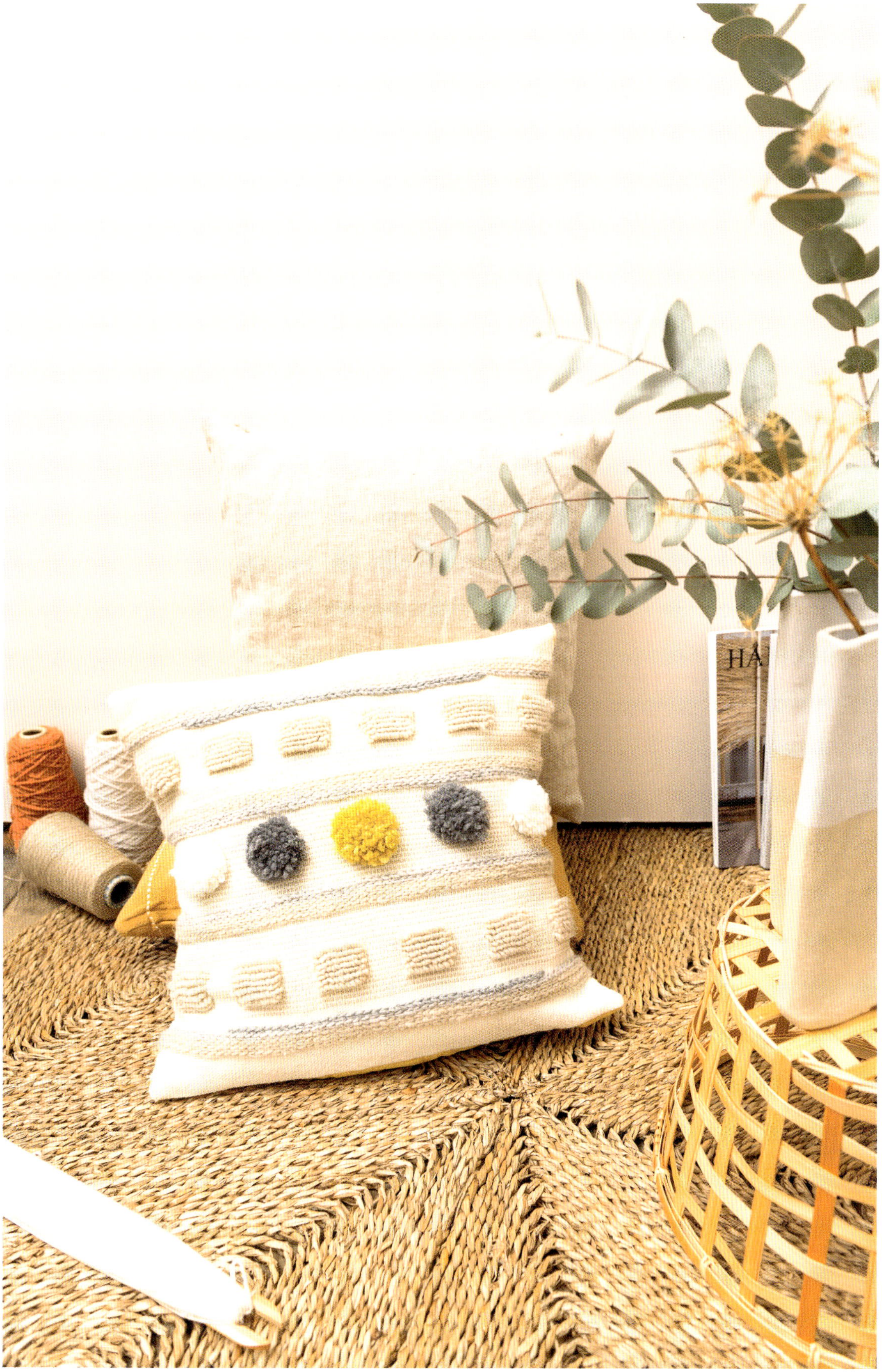

Instructions

1 Wind on a warp 20 in. wide by 31½ in. long (50 × 80 cm) with the Yaku yarn in Rahvid, using a 12.5-dent (50/10) heddle. Carefully center your warp on the loom.

2 After evening out the warp with thick cotton yarn, prepare 4 shuttles with the Woolly yarn in Sand, Pigeon, and Shadow, as well as the Økologisk Hverdagsuld yarn.

3 Cut fringe about 2 in. (5 cm) long for the rya knots in the Woolly Sand, Pigeon, and Shadow colorways, as well as the Økologisk Hverdagsuld wool.

4 Work about 2⅜ in. (6 cm) in plain weave with the Økologisk Hverdagsuld wool.

5 Start to weave the soumak with the Økologisk Hverdagsuld. Place the heddle in the neutral position and work the soumak stitch back and forth. Stabilize the soumak with 2 rows of plain weave using the same yarn.

6 Weave two more back and forth rounds in soumak with the Woolly Sand, one round with Pigeon and one round with Shadow. Always use the Økologisk Hverdagsuld wool for the plain weave between the different soumak stitches to stabilize them.

7 Work ⅜ in. (1 cm) in plain weave with the Økologisk Hverdagsuld.

8 Work ¾ in. (2 cm) in plain weave, alternating 1 row of Woolly Sand and 2 rows of Økologisk Hverdagsuld.

9 Start working the loops with the Woolly Sand. Make 6 loop squares, 2 in. (5 cm) wide, spaced 1¼ in. apart. To do this, pass the Sand color shuttle from right to left. Using your knitting needle, pull loops up through the warp threads, sliding them over your needle as you go. Start the first square 1 in. (3 cm) from the edge, *pull up loops for 2 in. (5 cm), leaving 1¼ in. (3 cm) without loops*. Repeat from * to * until you have 6 squares of loops on your needle. Beat.

10 Work 2 rows of plain weave with the Økologisk Hverdagsuld wool, continuing to keep the needle in place. Don't remove it until the second row has been completed, when the loops are stabilized.

11 Repeat steps 9 and 10 until you have 7 rows of loops.

12 Work 1¼ in. (3 cm) of plain weave, alternating 1 row of Woolly Sand and 2 rows of Økologisk Hverdagsuld.

13 Work 4 rows in soumak stitch with the Woolly yarn: 2 rows in Sand and 2 rows in Pigeon. Always use Økologisk Hverdagsuld wool to work plain weave between Soumak stitches to stabilize them.

14 Work 1¼ in. (3 cm) of plain weave, alternating 1 row of Woolly Sand and 2 rows of Økologisk Hverdagsuld.

15 Work the first row of rya knots. This row will contain 5 pom-poms, 2 in. (5 cm) in diameter and 2 in. (5 cm) apart. You'll use Woolly yarn in Cream, Shadow, and Sulphur for the pom-poms. Start 2 in. (5 cm) from the edge and, for the first row, tie *3 knots per pom-pom and skip 2¼ in. (6 cm)*. Repeat from * to * across the entire width. Work 1 row in plain weave with the Økologisk Hverdagsuld.

16 Make the second row of knots, this time 5 knots per pom-pom, again with the same alternating colors. Work 1 row in plain weave with the Økologisk Hverdagsuld.

17 Make the third row of knots, now with 7 knots per pom-pom. Work 1 row in plain weave with the Økologisk Hverdagsuld.

18 Repeat step 17, then step 16, and finally step 15 to finish the pom-poms.

Good to Know
You are now halfway through your pillow; the rows will now be repeated in mirror image.

19 Repeat steps 12 to 14, then 9, 8, 7, and 6. Finish by working about 2¼ in. (6 cm) in plain weave with the Økologisk Hverdagsuld wool.

20 Cut your piece from the loom at the top, leaving 4-inch (10 cm) lengths of thread and tie temporary knots to keep it from unraveling while being moved.

21 Unwind your weave from the front beam. Untie the knots at the beginning and remove the thick cotton yarn used to even out the warp. Tie temporary knots to keep it from unraveling while being moved.

22 Secure both ends with a zigzag stitch or with a serger.

23 Trim the yarn on the rya knots to shorten and give the pom-poms a rounded shape.

24 Wash the woven fabric, dry flat, and iron gently on the reverse side.

25 Cut your fabric to the same size as the weave to make the back of the pillow. Stitch the two pieces together on three sides, ⅜ in. (1 cm) from the edge, right sides together.

26 Turn the fabric right side out through the open side and sew this side closed by hand after inserting your pillow. You could also attach buttons or a zipper to create a removable cover.

Pair of Placemats

This lively project will brighten up your table! These sets are an easy introduction to using the pick-up stick and weaving weft and warp floats.

Once you understand the principle, new horizons are opened up and it's easy to create your own patterns on the rigid heddle loom. What's more, as you only have to change the pick-up stick three times per placemat, this project moves along surprisingly fast.

Technique: Float patterns worked with a pick-up stick (page 75)
Sett: 10 ends per inch (4 threads/cm)
Warping dimensions: 13 in. × 43 in. (32 × 110 cm)
Final dimensions: 2 placemats, 11 in × 15 in. (28 × 38 cm) each, including hems

Difficulty: Advanced
Time required: 8 hours
Sewing: Hem, can do by hand

Tools and Materials
- Loom + warping materials (page 24)
- 4 shuttles
- Pick-up stick
- Needle

Yarn
Sandnes Garn Mandarin Petit
- Warp: 2 skeins White
- Weft:
  - 1½ skeins White (used as single yarn)
  - 1 skein Chili (used doubled)
  - 1 skein Almond (used doubled)
  - 1 skein Mint (used doubled)

Notes
- To give the floats more impact, I've doubled the colored threads, while the basic white thread is used in single thickness.
- Warp exactly 128 threads to make the pattern work.
- When working the plain weave between rows of float patterns, make sure to always alternate up and down reed positions. To help you remember where you are in the pattern, apply my tip: In the heddle's up position, always pass the shuttle from right to left, and in the down position, pass it from left to right.
- If you don't have a sewing machine or serger for hemming, you can use the hemstitch to secure the hem.

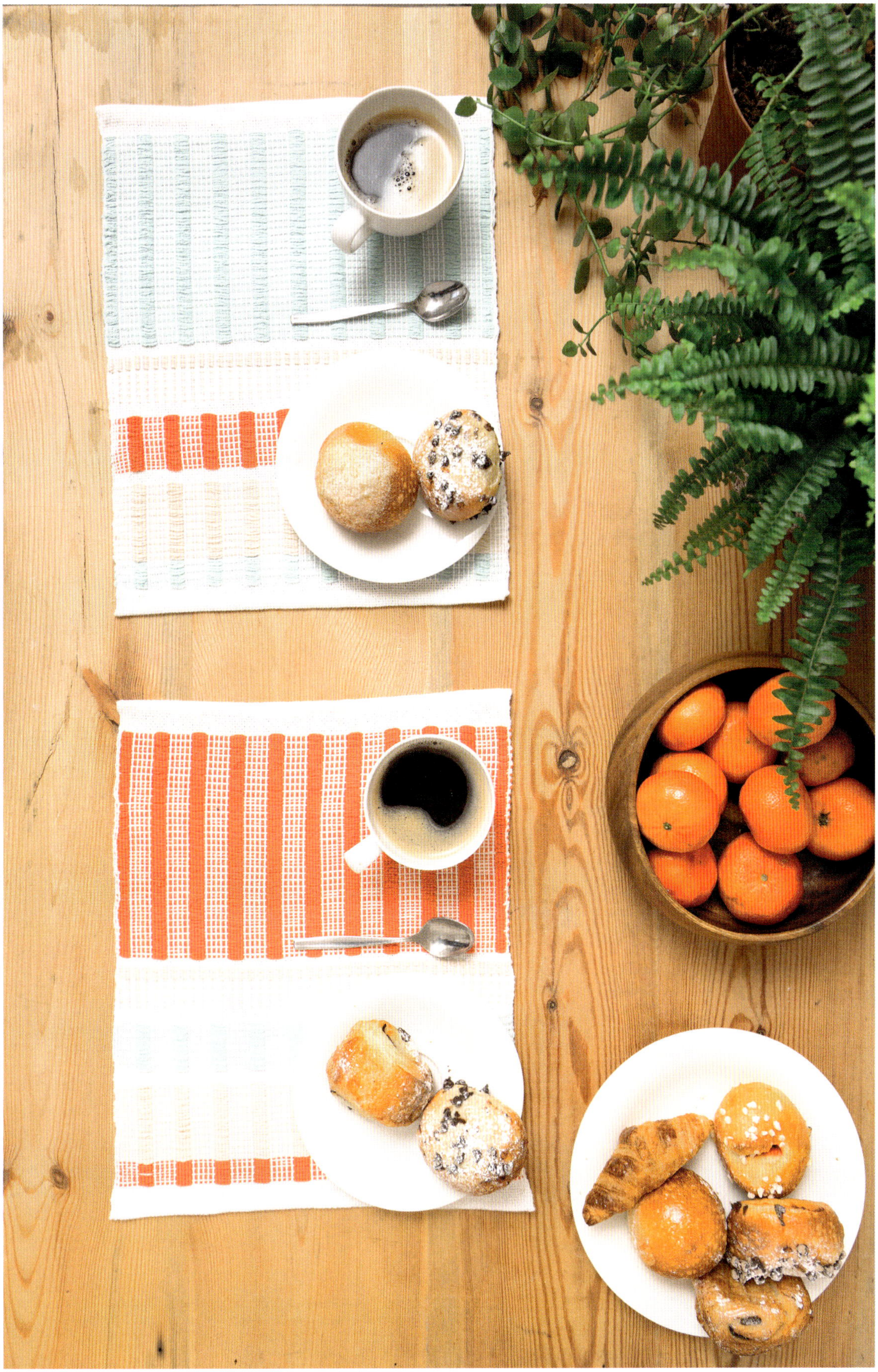

Instructions

1 Wind on a warp 12¾ inches wide by 43 inches long (30 × 110 cm) with White, using a 10-dent (40/10) heddle. Carefully center your warp on the loom. Be sure that you have 128 warp ends (and therefore 64 slots).

2 After evening out the warp with thick cotton yarn, prepare a shuttle with White. For the three other colors, prepare the shuttles by doubling the yarn. Take the two ends of your first skein and wind the yarn around the shuttle as if they formed a single yarn. The two strands of yarn will be woven together.

Placemat 1

Hemstitch

If you want to do a hemstitch (see page 43), leave a tail of at least 27 in. (70 cm) of White thread at the beginning of the weave. Work 4 rows in plain weave then thread the tail through the needle to make the hemstitch.

3 Work about 2 in. (5 cm) in plain weave with the White.

4 Place the heddle in the down position and insert the pick-up stick behind the heddle in the following sequence: 1 thread over, *3 threads under, 4 threads over*. Repeat from * to * until the last warp end, and finish with 1 thread over.

5 Create weft floats as described in the following steps.

- **Place the heddle in the neutral position**, slide the pick-up stick to the back of the heddle and turn it on the edge. This will open a new shed in front of the heddle. Insert your Chili color weft. Turn the pick-up stick flat and return it to the back of the loom to close the new shed.
- Place the heddle in the up position and weave with White weft from right to left.
- **Place the heddle in the neutral position**, slide the pick-up stick to the back of the heddle and turn it on edge to open a new shed. Insert your shuttle with the Chili yarn before turning the pick-up stick flat and returning it to the back of the loom.

- Place the heddle in the down position and weave a pick with the White weft from left to right.

Repeat these instructions over 6¼ in. (16 cm), always alternating 1 pattern row in Chili with the pick-up stick and 1 row of plain weave in White. Finish with 4 rows of plain weave in White.

6 Place the heddle in the down position, remove the pick-up stick from the warp, and then use it to create another pattern: 1 thread up, *1 thread down, 1 thread up*; repeat along the entire weft.

7 Repeat step 5 for ⅜ in. (1 cm), replacing the Chili yarn with the Almond yarn. Continue to always alternate 1 pattern row with the pick-up stick in color and 1 row of plain weave in White for ⅜ in. (1 cm).

8 Create warp floats.

Please Note

For the next ¾ in. (2 cm), the use of the pick-up stick changes.

- Place the heddle in the **up position**, slide the pick-up stick to the back of the heddle and **leave it flat**! This will open up a new shed in front of the heddle. Insert the shuttle with the Almond yarn. Return the pick-up to the back of the loom to close the new shed.
- Leave the heddle in the up position and pass the shuttle with the White weft from right to left.
- Leave the heddle in the up position, slide the pick-up stick to just behind the heddle and leave it flat. This will open a new shed in front of the heddle. Insert your shuttle with the Almond colorway before returning the pick-up stick flat to the back of the loom to close the new shed.
- Place the heddle in the down position and pass the shuttle with the White weft from left to right.

Repeat these operations for ¾ in. (2 cm), alternating 1 row of pattern with the pick-up stick in Almond and 1 row of plain weave in White. Finish with 4 rows of plain weave in White.

9 Place the heddle in the down position and remove the pick-up stick from the warp to create another pattern: 5 threads up, *3 threads down, 4 threads up*, repeat from * to * all along the weft and finish with 5 threads up.

10 Repeat step 5, using the Mint colorway for 2 in. (5 cm), then the Chili yarn for the next ¾ in. (2 cm). Always alternate 1 row of pattern in colors with the pick-up stick and 1 row of plain weave in White. Finish with ⅜ in. (1 cm) of plain weave in White.

11 Repeat step 5, using the Mint colorway for 2 in. (5 cm), then the Chili for the next ¾ in. (2 cm). Always alternate 1 row of pattern in color with the pick-up stick and 1 row of plain weave in White. Finish with 2 in. (5 cm) of plain weave in White.

The first placemat ends here.

Hemstitch

If you want to do the hemstitch, do it at this point to secure the end of the first placement.

----

12 Weave a stripe at least 1¼ in. (3 cm) long with the White yarn, which will allow you to cut apart the two placemats when the weave is done.

Placemat 2

13 Follow steps 1 to 11 above. The only difference is in the thread colors. Switch the Chili and Mint colorways, but the patterns remain the same.

Separating and Finishing Placemats

14 Cut your piece from the loom at the top, leaving 1¼ in. (3 cm) if you've opted for the hemstitch. Otherwise, leave 2 to 2½ in. (5 or 6 cm) of thread before tying temporary knots to keep it from unraveling while being moved.

15 Unwind your placemats from the front beam. Untie the knots at the beginning and remove the thick cotton yarn used to even out the warp.

16 Separate the two placemats by cutting down the middle of the white stripe.

17 If you did not do a hemstitch, secure the two ends of both placemats with a zigzag stitch.

18 Wash the placemats in hot water, lay flat to dry, and iron.

19 Double hem both ends of each placemat. Fold the first end of the dish towel over ⅜ in. (1 cm) from right side to back side and iron the fold. Fold the same edge over ⅜ in. (1 cm) and iron, again from right side to back side. Pin the hem along its entire length before machine or hand-stitching with a blindstitch. Repeat on the second end.

20 Iron your placemats, especially the hems.

Large Woven Trivet

Here is an unusual project. The insertion of thin wood dowels makes it unique and playful. Easy enough to do if you've already practiced with the pick-up stick, this technique is always good to know.

Technique: Supplemental warp (page 82)
Sett: 10 ends per inch (4 threads/cm)
Warping dimensions: 13½ in. × 32 in. (32 × 80 cm)
Final dimensions: 12 in. × 20 in. (30 × 50 cm)

Difficulty: Intermediate
Time required: 6 hours
Sewing: Hem, sewn by hand

Tools and Materials
- Loom + warping materials (page 24)
- Shuttle
- Pick-up stick
- 45 natural wood dowels: diameter ⅛ in. (3 mm), 12 in. (30 cm) long
- Needle

Yarn
Gist Yarn Beam 3/2 Organic Cotton Weaving Yarn
- Warp:
  - Main warp: 1 bobbin Jade
  - Supplemental warp: 1 bobbin Tangerine
- Weft: 1 bobbin Jade

Notes
- For the pattern to work, warp exactly 134 threads (i.e., 67 slots).
- The technique is explained in detail on page 82, but here is a quick summary. After loading 13 in. (33 cm) of conventional warp on the loom, insert the supplemental warp threads above each of the strands at the desired points. In some slots, you will have 4 threads instead of 2. Wind the supplemental warp with the main warp. **However, leave these supplemental warp ends in the slots, do not pull them through the eyes in the next step!**
- Insert the pick-up stick behind the heddle, underneath all the supplemental warp threads.
- During weaving, sliding the pick-up stick directly behind the heddle will lift the supplemental warp and exclude it from the shed. This will create floats. When the pick-up stick is pushed to the back of the loom, the supplemental warp is woven with the other warp ends.

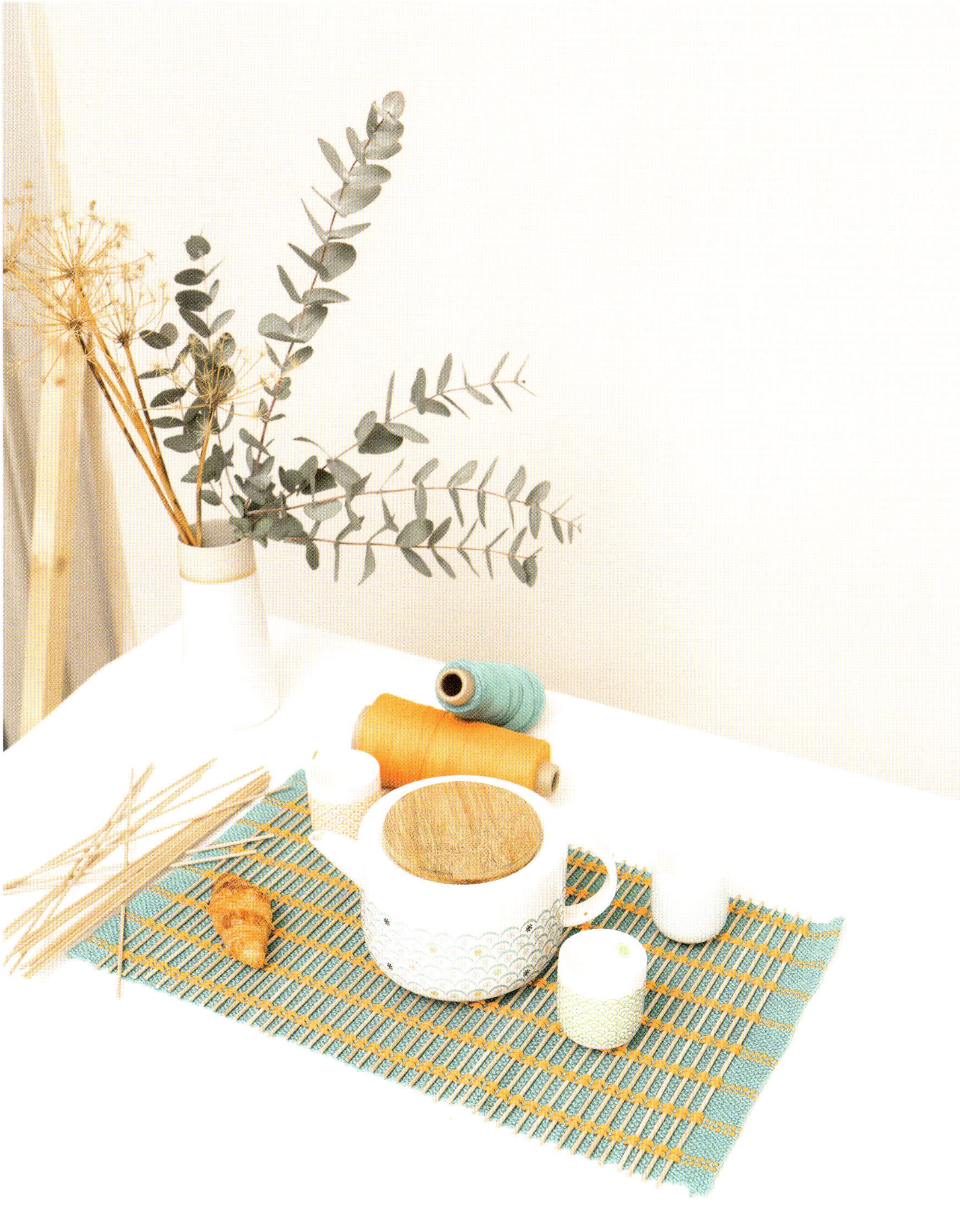

Instructions

1 Wind on a warp 13½ in. (32 cm) wide and 32 in. (80 cm) long using a 10-dent (40/10) heddle and Jade yarn. Make sure you have exactly 134 warp ends. Carefully center your warp on the loom.

2 After threading the slots with the Jade yarn, but before cutting and winding the layer of warp, add the supplemental warp threads.

- Attach the Tangerine yarn to the back bar, ¾ in. (2 cm) to the left of the first Jade thread.
- Using the threading hook, pull this thread through the 6th slot in the fabric, just above the Jade thread, then slide the thread around the warping peg.
- Pull the thread a second time through the 7th slot above the Jade thread and slide it around the warping peg.
- Cut the Tangerine yarn and tie the end around the back rod.
- Leave 7 slots with no Tangerine yarn. Tie it on the rod again opposite the 8th slot and pull the thread through the slot.

Continue in this way, always leaving 7 slots free between 2 slots threaded with the supplemental Tangerine color thread. At the end, you should have 8 × 2 slots with the Tangerine yarn above the Jade yarns.

3 Continue warping as usual, but do not place the supplement warp threads in the eyes; leave them in the slots.

4 After evening out the warp with a thick cotton yarn, prepare 1 shuttle with the Jade color yarn.

Hemstitch

If you want to do the hemstitch, work 4 rows in plain weave, leaving a tail at least 32 in. (80 cm) long at the start of the weave, then thread it through a needle to work the hemstitch.

---

5 Work 2 in. (5 cm) in plain weave with Jade.

6 Insert the pick-up stick behind the heddle, under all the supplemental warp threads.

7 Create floats and insert the wood dowels.

- **Place the heddle in the neutral position**, slide the pick-up stick to just behind the heddle (no need to turn it on edge). This will raise the supplemental warp and create a float into which you insert the wooden dowel.
- Place the heddle in the up position, leave the pick-up stick in front, and make a pass with the Jade weft.
- Place the heddle in the down position, still leaving the pick-up stick in front, and make a second pass with the Jade weft.
- Place the heddle in the down position, push the pick-up stick to the back of the loom and pass the Jade weft.
- Move the heddle to the up position, leave the pick-up stick in the back, and make a second pass with the Jade weft.

Pattern Repeat

- 1 row with heddle in neutral position, pick-up stick up front + insert wood,
- 2 rows of plain weave with pick-up stick in front,
- 2 rows of plain weave with pick-up stick in back.

Repeat these steps for 18 in. (46 cm), gradually inserting 45 little wood dowels as you go.

8 Work 2 in. (5 cm) in plain weave with Jade.

Hemstitch

If you want to do a hemstitch, leave a yarn tail of at least 27 in. (70 cm) at the end of the weave, then thread a needle to work the stitch.

9 Cut your piece off the loom at the top, leaving 1¼ in. (3 cm) if you've opted to do the hemstitch. Otherwise, leave 2 to 2¼ in. (5 to 6 cm) of thread before making temporary knots to keep it from unraveling while being moved.

10 Unwind your woven fabric from the front warp beam. Untie the knots from the beginning and remove the thick cotton yarn used to even out the warp.

11 If you haven't done a hemstitch, secure both ends of the trivet with a zigzag stitch.

12 Iron the trivet on the reverse side.

13 Double hem both ends of the fabric. Fold the first end over ⅜ in. (1 cm) from right side to back side and iron the fold. Fold the same edge over ⅜ in. (1 cm), again from right side to back side, and iron. Pin the hem along its entire length before machine stitching. Repeat on the second end.

Large Woven Trivet - 139

Pair of Coasters

Although these coasters are the smallest woven items presented here, they are also the most time-consuming and most difficult to make! The technique is based on the overshot technique normally used on multi-shaft looms. You weave with two different thread thicknesses: a thinner thread for the background fabric and a thicker one for the pattern. The threads must alternate: one pass with the fine thread and one pass with the pattern thread.

The pattern is created with a pick-up stick, row by row. While the process allows complete freedom in creating the pattern, it is very time-consuming.

Technique: Overshot (page 84)
Sett: 12.5 ends per inch (5 threads/cm)
Warping dimensions: 5½ in. × 27½ in. (14 × 70 cm)
Number of warp ends: 72
Final dimensions of a coaster: 4¼ in. × 8 in. (11 × 20 cm), including fringe

Difficulty: Advanced
Time required: 12 hours
Sewing: No

Tools and Materials
- Loom + warping materials
- 2 shuttles
- 1 pick-up stick
- Needle

Yarn
- Warp: Sandnes Garn Mandarin Petit, 1½ skeins White
- Weft:
  - Sandnes Garn Mandarin Petit, 1½ skeins White (for plain weave)
  - Gist Yarn Beam 3/2 Organic Cotton Weaving Yarn, 1 bobbin Jade
  - Gist Yarn Beam 3/2 Organic Cotton Weaving Yarn, 1 bobbin Tangerine

Notes
- For the pattern to work, warp exactly 72 threads: 70 for the pattern and 2 selvedge threads.
- This technique requires a lot of patience. Before using it in a larger project, it is best to test it with these small coasters.
- When working the plain weave between the float pattern rows, make sure you always alternate the up and down positions of the heddle. To remember where you are, apply my tip: When the heddle is up, pass the shuttle right to left, and when the heddle is down, always pass it left to right. Following the pattern diagram already requires concentration; without a simple way to see where you are in the plain weave, you'll soon be lost.
- There are many more beautiful, advanced patterns to be found in Myra Wood's book *Crazyshot*.

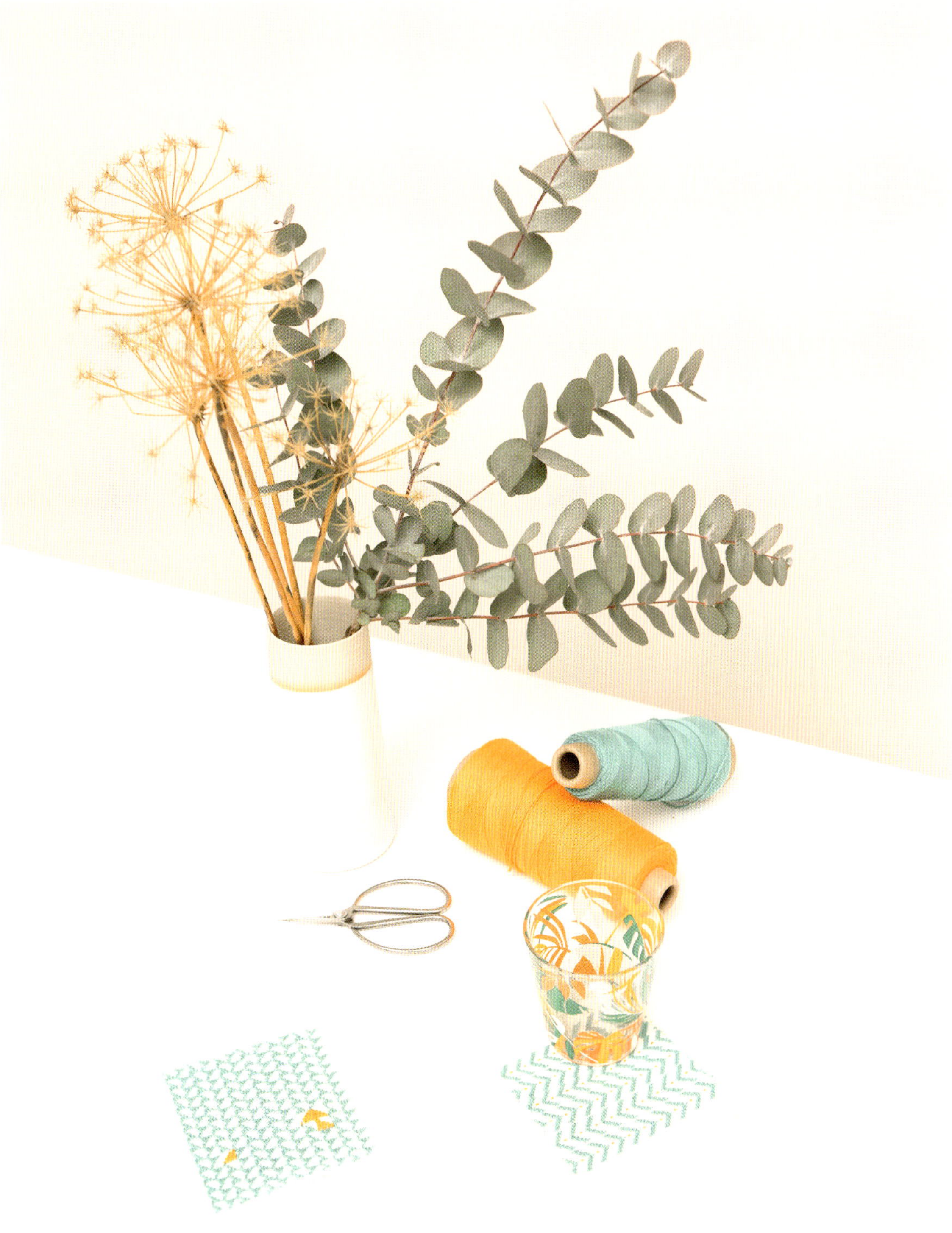

Instructions

1 Wind on a warp 5½ in. (14 cm) wide and 27½ in. (70 cm) long using a 12.5-dent (50/10) heddle. Make sure you have exactly 72 warp ends, i.e., 36 slots (as there are always 2 threads per slot). Carefully center your warp on the loom.

2 After evening out the warp with thick cotton yarn, prepare 1 shuttle with the Jade yarn and 1 with White.

Coaster 1

3 Work the first 4 rows in plain weave with White, leaving a tail at least 20 in. (50 cm) long at the beginning of the weave.

4 Thread the end of this yarn through the needle and hemstitch (see page 43).

5 Continue working in plain weave with White for ¾ in. (2 cm) to create the bottom border. Finish with 1 row with the heddle in the down position.

6 Place the heddle in neutral position. Take the pick-up stick and start inserting it in front of the heddle following the first line of diagram 1 on page 143. Turn it on edge to open the pattern shed and slide in the Jade shuttle to weave the first row. Remove the pick-up stick.

....

Good to Know

The first and last rows are not part of the pattern.

....

7 Place the heddle in the up position and work 1 row of plain weave with White.

8 Repeat steps 6 and 7, alternating the up and down heddle positions as described in the Notes, until you have woven all the rows in diagram 1 (see page 143).

9 Some rows contain a second color (Tangerine) and require a special technique. To complete these rows, use the overshot principle.

When using the pick-up stick to make a row containing two colors, treat the squares of the second color as white squares, meaning you pass the pick-up stick under the warp threads representing these squares to avoid superimposing two weft threads. After having passed through your shuttle with the Jade, cut a short piece of the Tangerine yarn. Thread it through a needle and set the heddle in the neutral position. Then insert the second color, following the diagram manually, as if embroidering.

10 Finish with ¾ in. (2 cm) of plain weave fabric in White, leaving a tail at least 20 in. (50 cm) long at the end of the weave. Weave the last row from left to right and thread the remaining tail through the needle to do a hemstitch.

The first coaster ends here.

11 Before starting on the second coaster, you need to leave at least 2¾ in. (7 cm) of warp free. This will allow for 1¼ in. (3 cm) of fringe at the top of the first fabric and 1¼ in. (3 cm) of fringe at the bottom of the second. The remaining ⅜ in. (1 cm) will be used to cut the two pieces in the middle.

To leave this space, you can either insert a 2¾ in. (7 cm) piece of cardboard between the two coasters, or weave 2¾ in. (7 cm) of plain weave with a very thick cotton (like the one used to even out the warp at the beginning, for example).

Coaster 2

12 Take some new White yarn and repeat steps 3 to 10, following diagram 2 (see page 144).

Separating and Finishing the Coasters

13 Cut the fabric from the loom at the top, leaving about 1½ in. (4 cm) of thread after the hemstitch. This hemstitch secures the weave, so there's no need to tie knots.

14 Unwind the front warp beam with your two coasters. Untie the knots at the beginning and remove the thick cotton used to even out the warp. Use a ruler to straighten the bottom of the fringe, leaving about 1¼ inches.

15 Wash coasters in hot water, lay flat to dry, and iron.

A Reminder on How to Read Diagrams

- The diagram shows only the pattern rows; the row of plain weave between the rows is not shown but must still be woven.
- The diagram is read from right to left and from bottom to top.
- Each column corresponds to a warp thread, each row to a weft pick.
- Pick-up stick row:
  - white box: pick-up stick goes below this warp thread,
  - colored box: pick-up stick goes above this warp thread.

Coaster 1 diagram

Pair of Coasters - 143

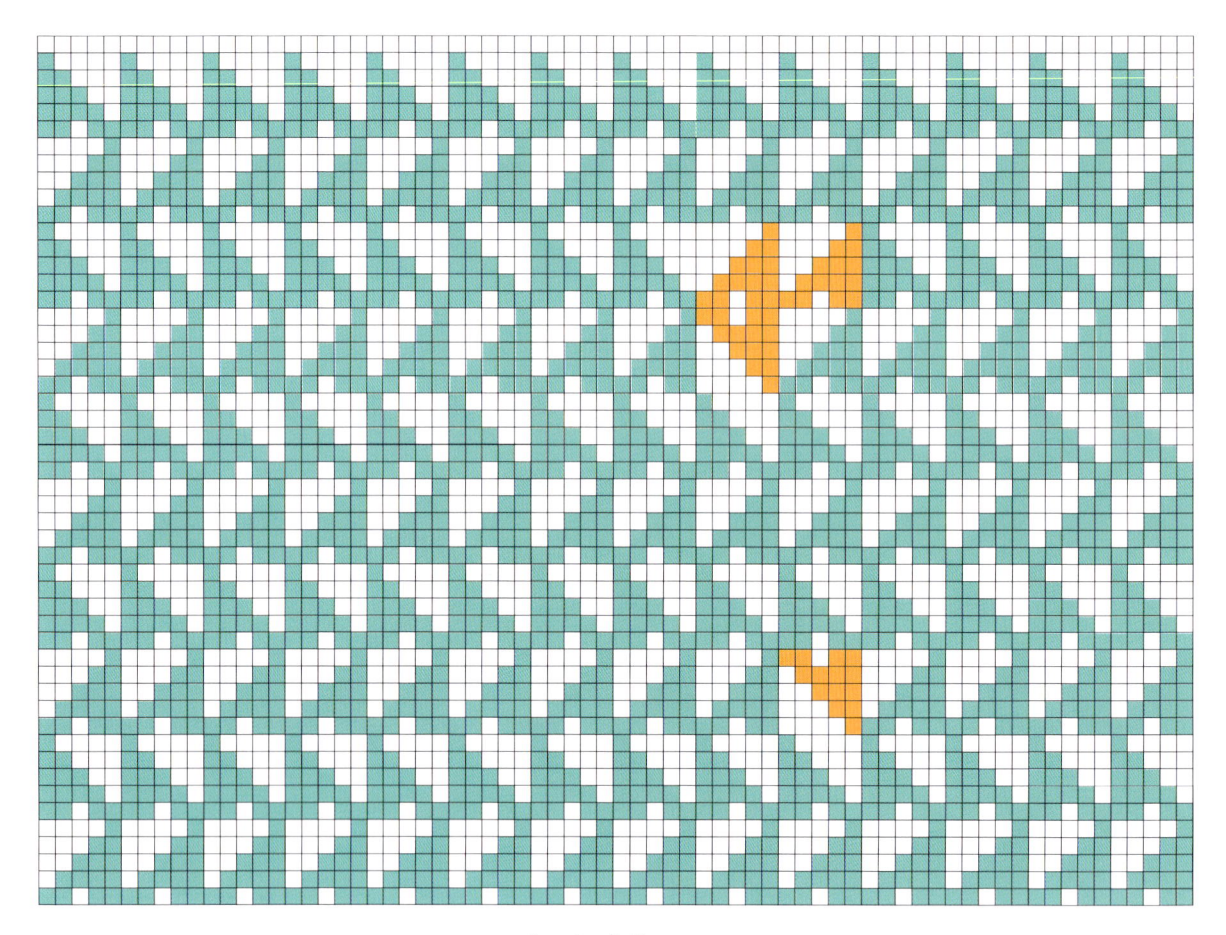

Coaster 2 diagram

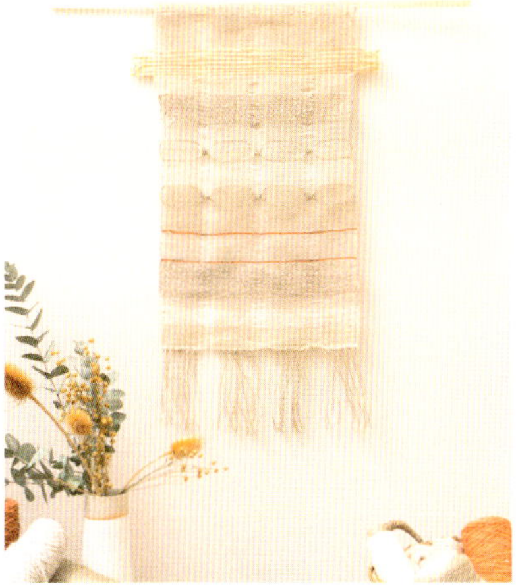
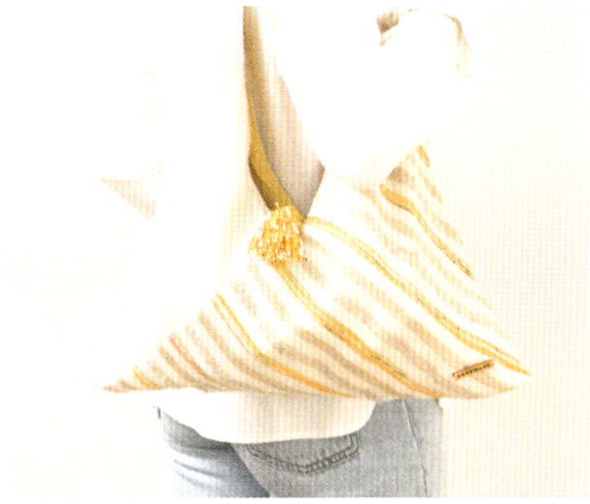
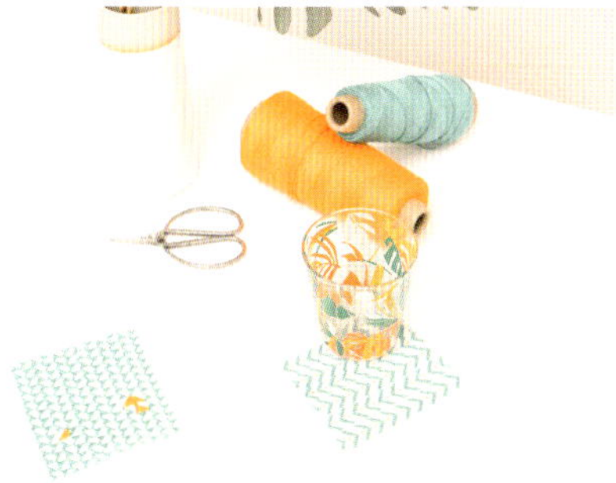
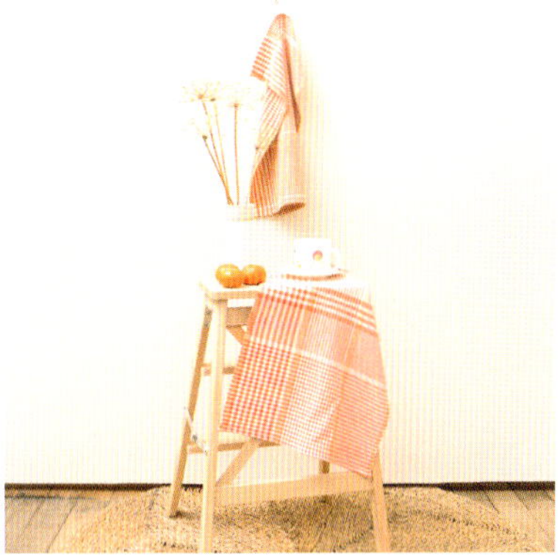
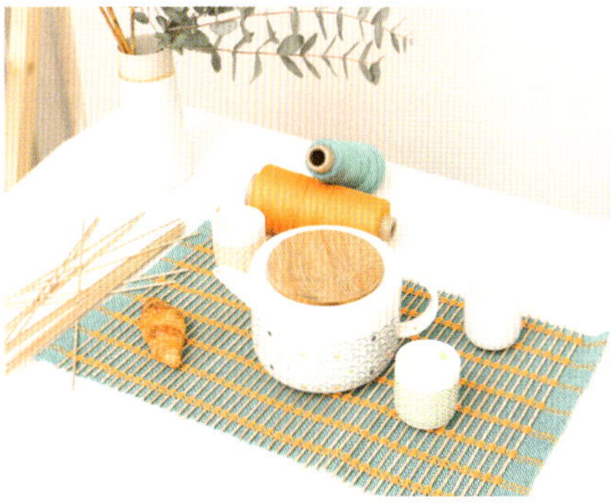
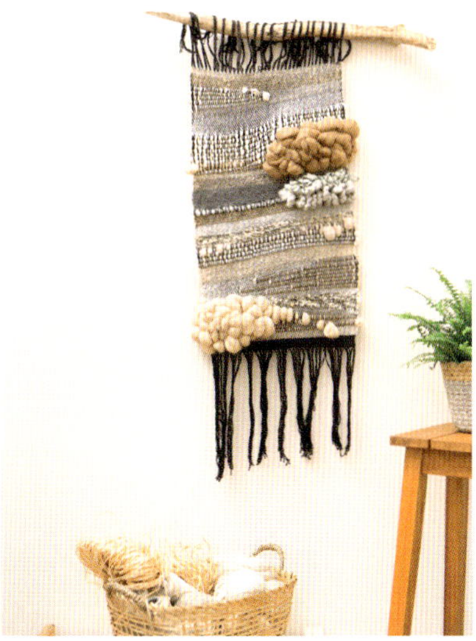
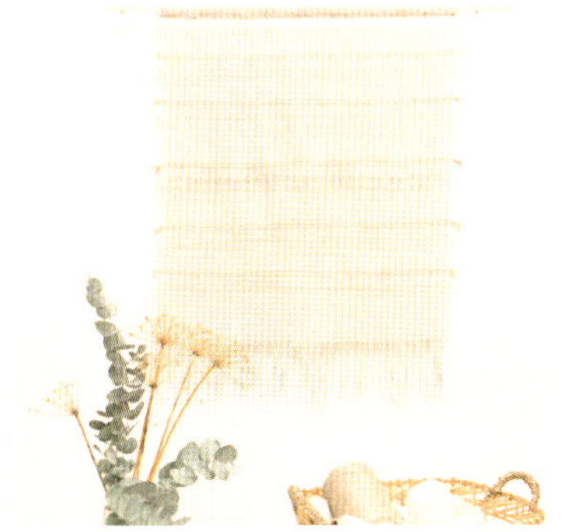
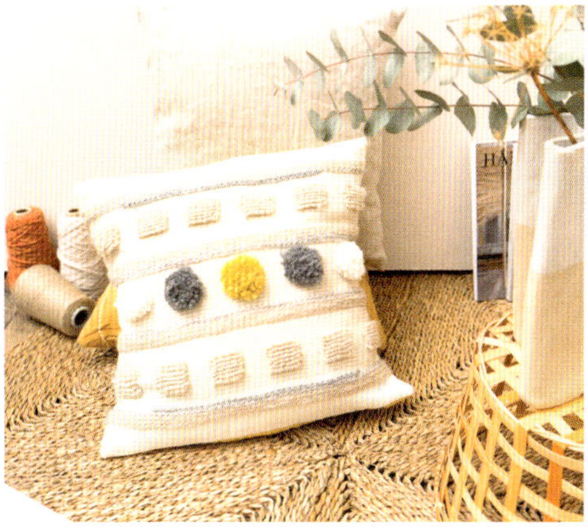
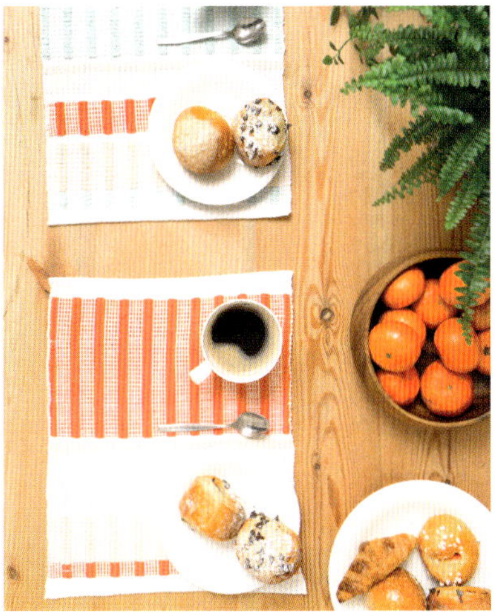
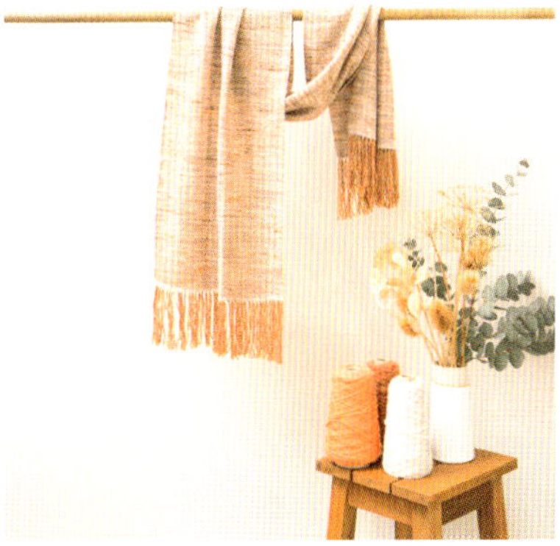
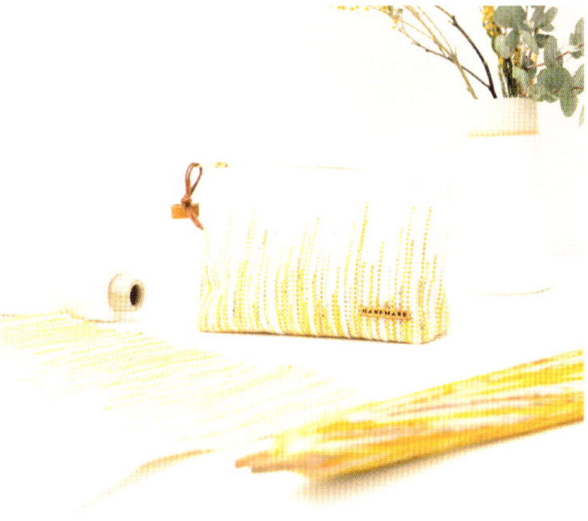

Glossary

Beams: Rollers on the front and back of the loom. The back beam is used to wind the warp, and the cloth is wound around the front beam as it is woven.

Beating: Action of pulling the heddle forward and pushing the last weft pick in place after each pass of the shuttle.

Clasped weft: Weaving technique in which two yarns are used at the same time. Each yarn comes from the opposite side of the weave and the two connect in the middle of the fabric.

Float: Thread that passes over several warp or weft threads in a row.

Overshot: Weaving pattern in which two different wefts are used, a thin weft for the ground weave, the base structural fabric, and a thicker weft to create a non-structural pattern on top.

Pick-up stick: Stick pointed on at least one side, inserted into the warp behind the heddle to create additional patterns.

Plain weave: Basic weave on the rigid heddle loom. The weft thread goes over one warp end and under the next, and in the next row it does the opposite.

Rigid heddle reed: Plastic part containing slots and eyes through which the warp passes. It is also used to beat the weft and to create density and patterns.

Selvedge: Fabric edge.

Sett: Number of ends per inch.

Shed: Opening between warp threads, created when the heddle position is changed (up/down).

Shrinkage: Reduction of the fabric size due to the weaving itself or to the treatment of the fabric once it has left the loom.

Shuttle: Tool used to pass the weft thread through the warp. There are several types, but they are usually made of wood. Flat shuttles are the type mainly used with rigid heddle looms.

Structure: Main fabric structure created by the interlacing of warp and weft threads, such as plain weave, twill, and satin. Plain weave is the main type of structure made on a rigid heddle loom.

Temple: Tool used to keep the fabric at its initial width. It is installed between the two selvedges of the fabric.

Threading hook: Hook used to pass the warp through the heddle. There are flat plastic ones and curved metal ones.

Twill: Basic weave structure characterized by diagonal lines and chevrons. It is not very common on a rigid heddle loom, as this weave normally requires four shafts.

Warp: A layer of yarn attached to the loom. The yarn is stretched between the two beams, passing through the heddle.

Warping: Action of attaching the warp to the loom. There is direct warping, most often used on a rigid heddle loom, or indirect warping, which requires an additional warping device.

Weft: The yarn used for weaving, which runs perpendicular to the warp.

Supplies and Resources

Alysse Creations
http://alysse-creations.info

Bart and Francis
Known especially for their somewhat special and rare fibers. I order horsehair here, for example.
https://bart-francis.be/fr/

CaMaRose
https://camarose.store/shop

DMC
https://www.dmc.com/US/en

Funem
I order all my materials for Saori and textured weaves here.
https://funemstudio.com/

Gistyarn
Supplies, yarn, and materials.
https://www.gistyarn.com/

Hedgehog Fibres
https://shop.hedgehogfibres.com

PaperPhine
https://shop.paperphine.com

Sandnes Garn
https://www.sandnes-garn.com/

Bibliography

Books

Davenport, Betty Linn, *Hands On Rigid Heddle Weaving*, Interweave, 1987.

Gipson, Liz, *Weaving Made Easy: 17 Projects Using a Simple Loom*, Interweave, 2008.

Hart, Rowena, *The Ashford Book of Rigid Heddle Weaving*, Ashford Handicrafts, 2008.

Mitchell, Syne, *Inventive Weaving on a Little Loom*, Storey Publishing, 2015.

Patrick, Jane, *The Weaver's Idea Book: Creative Cloth on a Rigid Heddle Loom*, Interweave, 2010.

Wood, Myra, *Crazyshot: Creative Overshot Weaving on a Rigid Heddle Loom*, independently published, 2021.

Magazines

The Wheel, Ashford's Fibrecraft Magazine, Issue 33, 2021–2022, Ashford Wheels and Looms.

Easy Weaving with Little Looms, Long Thread Media, Fall 2022.

Technical Table of Contents

Introducing the Rigid Heddle Loom

The Rigid Heddle Loom **8**
Advantages 8
Disadvantages 8
Key Words to Know 8
What Is a Rigid Heddle Loom? 10
Basic Tools 12
Tools to Go Further 13

Yarn **14**
A Variety of Materials 14
Natural Fibers of Animal Origin *14*
   Wool 14
   Silk 15
Natural Fibers from Plants *16*
   Cotton 16
   Flax (Linen) 17
   Hemp 17
Artificial and Synthetic Fibers *18*
Yarn Construction 18
Choosing Your Warp Yarn 19
Choosing Your Weft Yarn 19

Preparing Your Weaving Project

Calculating Density and Yardage **20**
Density 20
Calculating Ideal Yarn Density *20*
Adapting Yarn Density According to Certain Criteria .. *21*
   Fabric Function 21
   Yarns Used 21
   Weave Structure 21
Checking Density with a Sample *21*
Quantity of Yarn Needed 22
Calculating Shrinkage *22*
   Weaving Shrinkage and Loom Waste 22
   Processing Shrinkage 22
   How It Works 22
Calculating the Length of Yarn Required *23*
   For the Warp 23
   For the Weft 23
In Conclusion *23*

Setting up the Loom

Direct Warping **24**
Secure the Loom and the Warping Peg 24
Attach Warp to the Back Rod 25
Thread Warp through the Heddle Slots 26
Tie and Cut the Warp 28
Wrap Yarn around the Back Warp Beam 29
Thread the Eyes 29
Tie Warp to the Front Rod 31
Even out the Warp to Start Weaving 32

Weaving with the Rigid Heddle Loom **33**
Loading the Shuttles 33
Creating the Shed 34
Weaving 34
Changing Yarn While Weaving 35
Advancing and Winding the Warp 35
Finishing the Weave 36
Removing the Woven Fabric from the Loom 36
When the Warp Is Finished *36*
Before the Warp Is Finished *37*

Troubleshooting and Finishing Touches

When Things Go Wrong **38**
Tension Is Not Good 38
Edges Are Not Sharp 38
Weft Is on an Angle 39
Shed Does Not Open Properly 39
Fabric Is Too Stiff or Too Loose 39
Yarn Breaks 40
Length of Fabric Woven Is Difficult to Estimate ... 42

Finishing Steps **43**
Securing the Weave 43
Hemstitch 43
At the Beginning of the Weave *43*
At the End of the Weave *44*
Fringe 46
Washing and Ironing 47
Serger 47

Hems	47
Single Hem	*47*
Double Hem	*48*
Bias Tape	48
Interfacing	48
Felting	48
Sewing	49

Various Weave Structures

Plain Weave and Variations	**52**
Playing with Yarn Choice	52
Colors	*52*
Multicolor Yarns	52
Different Colors or Textures in Warp and Weft	52
Stripes	53
Checks	53
Textures	*53*
Handspun Wools	53
Yarns with Different Textures or Materials	53
Combining Smooth and Rustic Yarns	54
Unusual yarns	54
Color Effects	54
Houndstooth	*54*
Log Cabin	*56*
Clasped Weft	56
Playing with Weave Effects	57
Spaced Warp and Weft or Different Densities in Warp and Weft	*57*
Predominant Weft or Warp	*58*
Weft Dominant	58
Warp Dominant	59
Focus on the Japanese Saori Technique	**60**
Other Types of Structures	**62**
Finger-Controlled Techniques	62
Openwork and Medallions	*62*
Leno	62
Brooks Bouquet	65
Danish Medallions	67
Textured Stitches	*70*
Soumak Stitch	70
Rya Knots	72
Weaving with a Pick-Up Stick	75
Inserting the Pick-Up Stick	*76*
How to Read a Weaving Pattern	*76*
Types of Floats	*77*
Weft Floats (abbreviation = pick-up stick)	77
Warp Floats (abbreviation = heddle up and pick-up stick)	77
Creating Floats	*77*
Patterns with Weft or Warp Floats	*78*
Weft Floats	78
Warp Floats	80
Combinations of Warp and Weft Floats	81
Designs with Inlays	*82*
Patterns with Supplemental Warp	*83*
Warping the Loom	83
Weaving with Supplemental Warp threads	83
Overshot-Style Patterns	*84*
Weaving with Two Pick-Up Sticks	*85*
Inserting Pick-Up Sticks	85
Honeycomb Pattern	85
Replacing One of the Pick-Up Sticks with a Heddle Rod	85
Weaving with Two Heddles	87
Finer fabrics	*87*
Twill	*88*
The Theo Moorman Technique	*89*
Double Weave	*90*
Weaving Two Separate Layers	*91*
Weaving Two Separate Layers with Dark Dominant Top	*91*
Weaving Two Separate Layers with Light Dominant Top	*91*
Weaving Two Connected Layers	*91*
Double-Width Weave Joined on One Side	91
Tube Weave Joined on Both Sides	91
Focus on the Norwegian Krokbragd Technique	**92**
Krokbragd with Two Heddles	93
Krokbragd with a Heddle, a Pick-Up Stick, and a Heddle Rod	94

The Author

Petra Marciniak is a modern weaver who lives and works in Annecy, France.

"I've been weaving, in one form or another, for six years. After spending several years working on a rigid heddle loom using my own hand-spun yarns, I gradually progressed to larger looms. Today, I create unique, hand-woven textiles for the home and office, including rugs, pillow covers, wall hangings, and lampshades. I believe that interior textiles play a major role in creating a sense of comfort and serenity in the home. They add a tactile element, bringing texture and warmth to any room, that no other type of artwork can offer.

"My work is inspired by traditional Scandinavian and Japanese weaving, combined with a modern, minimal color palette. I use only high-quality natural fibers to create lasting heirlooms."